BEADAZZLED

BEADAZZLED

THE STORY OF BEADS

CHRIS & JANIE FILSTRUP

With line drawings by Loren Bloom

FREDERICK WARNE
New York   London

Frederick Warne & Co., Inc.
New York, New York

Library of Congress Cataloging in Publication Data
Filstrup, Chris.
Beadazzled—the story of beads.
Includes index.
Summary: Discusses the use of beads throughout history
as currency, ornaments, documents, and as aids in meditation
and mathematics. Also suggests beadwork projects.
1. Beads (in religion, folk-lore, etc.)—Juvenile
literature. 2. Beads—Juvenile literature.
[1. Beads. 2. Beadwork] I. Filstrup, Janie.
II. Title.
GT2250.F54   394   81-3426
ISBN 0-7232-6204-7   AACR2

Printed in the U.S.A. by The Murray Printing Company
Book Design by Kathleen Westray

1 2 3 4 5 85 84 83 82 81

TO EMMA AND BURTON

CONTENTS

ACKNOWLEDGMENTS

Special thanks to Jean Druesedow, fashion historian; Margaret Fife, beader; Edward Filstrup, engineer; Yoshiko Kawakatsu, financier; Phoebe Merrill, gardener; Alice Mertens, anthropologist; and J. A. Nip, landscape architect.

In addition, the authors would like to thank the following for their enthusiastic help in preparing this book:

E. H. Bigalke, director, East London Museum, South Africa
L. J. Botha, lecturer, University of Stellenbosch, South Africa
Hollywood Florists, Yonkers, New York
Metropolitan Museum of Art Costume Institute
Lilly Millard's Bead-L-Caravan, New York
I. Sherwin, director, Sheru Enterprises Inc., New York
Sweet Jar Terrarium Tools, San Jose, California

INTRODUCTION

The word "bead" comes from the Old English "bidden"—to pray. Long ago rich men and women established poorhouses that provided free room and board. In return, inmates were required to pray for the souls of the founders. Saying the prayers over and over, the residents of a poorhouse kept count on necklaces strung with small, perforated balls.

Gradually "bidden" became "bead," referring to the balls by which poor beadsmen and beadswomen counted their prayers. Then over the years "bead" came to mean any perforated globe counter and, finally, any small object that can be strung and hung.

Beads are most often round spheres or cylinders, but they may also be cubes, stars, or irregular shapes. Shells, teeth, seeds, gemstones, coral, metals, and glass are all bead-making materials. The Egyptians made some of their earliest beads of granite, and beads today may be of molded plastic, papier-mâché, or even denim cloth.

In New York City, the two blocks on 36th and 37th streets between Fifth and Sixth avenues are the wholesale bead capital of the United States. Store after store sells thousands of varieties of beads. In their windows, baskets, jars, and dishes overflow with beads from every part of the world. Inside the stores, little drawers, each with a sample bead tied to its handle, line the walls. Here you can find seed beads in a dozen shades of blue, or large multicolored beads from Venice. Some shops carry imported specialty beads, like fish bone, monkey bone, clamshell, bauxite, ivory, cowrie, and coconut shell from Africa; Egyptian scarabs; and lacquered cinnabar beads from China.

Beads are big business just off Fifth Avenue, but they are also the materials of people's crafts, adornment, money, and religious practices. *Beadazzled* is the story of beads, the important things they tell about how people have lived in the past and how they live now. Also included are craft projects that will help you learn about beads with your own hands. Like the Zulus of South Africa, you can design your own jewelry. Or make a bowdrill, an abacus, or a beaded rose! Some projects are easy, some very hard. Several are fun to do with a friend. All enable you to make something truly beautiful and fascinating to use or wear.

Less costly than gemstones, beads have been called poor people's jewels. Yet they can be fabulously elaborate works of art. Whether used for counting or courting, adorning or adoring, beads have caught people's fancy in almost every land, in almost every age. Beads are easy to own, fun to string, and pretty to see.

BEADAZZLED

JEWELS OF GLASS

1 When we think of ancient Egypt, the first things that come to mind are large—pyramids, the sphinx, the Nile River. In the nineteenth century, archaeologists excited people around the world by uncovering large Egyptian temples, cemeteries, and royal tombs. In looking for these big finds, early Egyptologists ignored the little objects of everyday life, or even destroyed them.

Around 1880, the Englishman Flinders Petrie changed all this. He turned excavating into a science. He taught excavators that little things can be just as important as large ones in showing us how ancient people lived. A sliver of bone might tell us as much as an entire mummy, or a bronze clasp as much as a box of jewels.

One of the small objects Petrie found and carefully preserved was a bead. He discovered it in an excavation layer dating from about 3500 B.C., and since Egyptologists had found glass objects from 1500 B.C., but no earlier, Petrie assumed that the perforated ball was quartz. This bead, Petrie thought, was far too old to be man-made glass. Then one day a curious friend saw that a small chip had fallen from the bead. He took it to a laboratory, where chemists found that the chip was made of silica, soda, and lime—the three ingredients of all glass. The bead was so beautifully made that it could not have been a first effort. By 3500 B.C., Petrie concluded, Egyptians either had been making beads for a long time or had borrowed glassmaking skills from others in the ancient Near East.

Since Petrie's discovery, other keen-eyed diggers have discovered simple glass beads made as early as 12,000 B.C. Till about 4000 B.C., these beads were not solid glass, but rather glass glaze covering a clay or stone core. Between 4000 and 3500 B.C., the Egyptians learned to make solid glass beads and to color them, sometimes with black and white stripes.

What exactly is glass? As we have said, glass is a mixture of sand (72 percent), soda (15 percent), lime (9 percent), and other minerals (4 percent). When heated in a furnace to at least eight hundred degrees Fahrenheit, the mixture melts and the three ingredients fuse into a molten mass.

The key ingredient of sand is silica, small crystals of quartz. The more silica in the sand, the clearer the glass. Soda lowers the melting point of silica and makes the molten metal even and smooth. Lime strengthens the glass as the metal cools. Without lime, glass would be too brittle for daily use.

Egyptians and other people of the Near East learned to color glass long before they could make it *translucent*, or clear enough to let light pass through. To the mix of sand, soda, and lime, they added cobalt to turn it blue, copper to turn it green, tin to turn it milky white, gold to turn it red. About 1600 B.C., glassmakers added manganese and saw that the mineral removed many of the impurities. When it cooled, the glass was translucent (but not transparent). Because of its cleaning properties, glassmakers still call manganese their soap.

Ancient Egyptians considered glass so beautiful that they valued it as highly as precious metals and gems. The most elegant royal jewelry used glass alongside semiprecious stones. King Tutankha- men's necklace of the sun is strung with beads of gold, carnelian, and glass. Carnelian and glass tip the wings of his vulture necklace. The loveliest piece of all, King Tut's great vulture collar that covered the dead pharaoh's chest, is inlaid with hundreds of pieces of colored glass. To us the glass looks like turquoise and lapis lazuli. To the royal craftsmen the imitation equaled the real thing. In fact, the ancient Egyptians invented the art of making fake jewels. They were so adept at giving glass color and texture that only a gem expert could tell the glass beads from pearls, emeralds, and tiger's eyes.

Egyptians made glass beads so well that pharaohs exported them all over the Near East. To control the bead industry and trade, pharaohs during the time of the Middle Kingdom (2130–1600 B.C.) built a large bead factory at Tell el Amarna, near Luxor. There bead-makers produced millions of beads for domestic use and export. From the pharaoh and his royal family down to merchants and farmers and even slaves, everybody wore them. Beads were not only attractive, they were sacred. The Egyptian hieroglyph for bead, *shasha*, also means luck. Most popular were beads decorated with colored eyes to protect the wearer from the evil eye, and beads of azure blue, the color of Hathor, queen of the heavens.

● The Egyptian hieroglyph *shasha,* meaning "bead."

shasha

In later times, beads in the shape of figs and other fruits were the fashion. In the time of Ramses III (1198–1167 B.C.), the conquering pharaoh, Egyptians wore beads shaped like the heads of foreign enemies. The factory at Tell el Amarna also produced enormous quantities of white cylinder beads that were sewn into nets used to wrap up mummies. The Pharaoh Tutmosis III, who ruled about 1480 B.C., himself worked in the factory and invented a rich hue of blue glass.

By 1200 B.C., the glassmakers of Egypt were making beads patterned with flowers, geometric designs, and human figures. The most complex patterns were made by fusing different-color rods of glass to make a larger rod. This rod was then reheated, twisted, and fused with other pieces of glass to produce dazzling designs. Flower beads reached their perfection in Alexandria in 300 B.C. but passed out of fashion under the Romans. Much later, about 1200 A.D., the glassmakers of Venice revived the art.

While the Egyptians manufactured the beads, the Phoenicians, who lived in present-day Lebanon, traded them abroad. When Egypt went into decline, about 500 B.C., the Phoenician glassmakers discovered for themselves how to blow glass and then how to make glass transparent. When Phoenicia fell under Roman rule, Phoenician glassmakers moved to Rome, where they made fine goblets and vases. But glass beads went out of style. For more than a thousand years, until the rise of Venice as a glassmaking center, glass beads were few, simple, and worn only by the poor. Romans and medieval Europeans with money preferred gold and silver and gems. Like many other crafts, glassmaking entered its own dark ages after the fall of Rome.

About 1200 A.D., Venice revived the art of making glass and became the glass capital of the world. One of the city's most famous citizens, Marco Polo, traveled to China and wrote about the silks and palaces and porcelains he saw there. But many more people traveled *to* Venice than *from* it. Usually they arrived by sea. If a traveler's lateener arrived at night, he would see a faint red glow over a section of the city and flaring red glows over the harbor island, Murano. These haloes came from the glassmaking shops, called glasshouses, whose furnaces were turned off only for infrequent repairs and for holidays. All night as well as all day, master craftsmen and their assistants worked twelve-hour shifts. Each glasshouse had a specialty. One made plates, another vases, yet another eyeglasses or mirrors. Many glasshouses. mostly on Murano, made beads.

The vases were graceful, the mirrors grand, the spectacles a miracle to the poor-sighted. But beads were the meat and potatoes of the glass industry. The merchants who traded in China, Sumatra, India, Baghdad, Africa, and later the New World, needed glass beads to exchange for silk, porcelain, spices, ivory, slaves, and beaver pelts.

Originally, all the glasshouses were in Venice proper. But in 1291, the council that governed the city ordered glasshouses with large furnaces to relocate on the harbor island of Murano, supposedly to protect the inhabitants of Venice from the fire hazard of the glass furnaces. True enough, a fire could break out in a glasshouse and spread quickly through the city. But the real reason for the move was to keep the secrets of glassmaking secret. Venetian glass was the best in the world because the master glassmakers had, by experiment, learned, first, the correct proportion of silica, salts, lime, and other minerals to make different kinds and colors of glass and, second, how to reheat and cool glass to make it strong. The penalty for revealing these secrets to anybody outside of Venice was death.

Of all the artisans of Venice—stonemasons, goldsmiths and silver-smiths, weavers, tailors, and the like—only the glassmakers were given the rank of burgher, or businessman, and allowed to marry daughters of noble families. Such alliances gave the glassmakers high status, but on Murano they lived like carefully watched pris-oners. The Committee of Ten, charged by the council to keep watch on the glassmakers, did not question a master glassmaker suspected of selling his secrets. It simply hired an assassin who in the dead of night stabbed the glassmaker to death and threw his body into a canal. "He was eaten by the salamander," the people of Murano would say, believing that a salamander, the animal sacred to the alchemist, lived in every glassmaking furnace.

At first the beadmakers formed one of five glassmakers' guilds. The other four guilds made bottles, mirrors, crystal, and glassware. The bead business grew so large that the beadmakers' guild split into two by specialty—small beads or large beads. Small beads were the ordinary single-colored beads that traders used as currency. Some large beads also went for trade, but most of them ended up in necklaces, earrings, and fancy rosaries. Later on, the rosary guild joined the beadmakers' guilds. The guilds controlled wages, terms of apprenticeship, quality of beads, and prices. Of the thousands of Venetian youth that wanted to join the beadmakers' guilds every year, only a few were chosen, these often sons of glassmakers.

Venetian beadmakers made beads in two ways. Beadmakers on Murano, where the government allowed large, very hot (between one thousand and fifteen hundred degrees Fahrenheit) furnaces, used the draw method. Each glasshouse had three furnaces shaped like beehives. The first and hottest melted the sand, soda, and lime and kept the mix molten in a basin called a crucible. The second furnace had several openings, called glory holes, into which the glassmakers put the glass shapes they were working on to reheat them for more shaping or for attaching to another piece of glass. The third furnace, the lehr, tempered the glass by slowly cooling it. This process, which could take several days, made the glass strong.

To make drawn beads, with an iron rod an assistant drew from the crucible of the first furnace a gob of molten glass, called the gather. He handed this to a master beadmaker, who rolled the gather on a slab of marble and worked it with long-handled pincers to shape it into a funnel, with the small end attached to the rod. By the time he had finished this shape—like a bottle without a bottom—the glass had cooled. So another assistant put the glass form into one of the glory holes of the second furnace until it turned white and soft. At just the right moment the assistant pulled the glass from

● "The Manufacture of Glass Beads" by Jacob van Loo, a seventeenth-century Dutch painter. The boy on the left is cutting cylinder beads from a drawn rod.

the furnace and handed it back to the master. A third assistant, called a runner, quickly fastened a second, thicker rod to the larger but collapsing end of the funnel. Then he ran, pulling the white-hot funnel into a long spaghetti of glass. The farther he ran, the thinner the spaghetti became. If the gather was large enough, about the size of a loaf of bread, and strong enough, a runner could draw out a spaghetti one hundred meters long. Because the original funnel was hollow, the spaghetti, no matter how long, stayed hollow.

When the master beadmaker judged the strand to be the correct thickness (one to twelve millimeters in diameter), the runner stopped. The two men carefully lay the long strand on the floor to cool. When ready, it was cut into meter-long lengths called canes. Young boys gathered the canes into sheaves and fed them into little guillotines that cut the canes into bead-size segments three to twelve millimeters long.

To strengthen the beads, the glassworkers stuffed their holes with a mixture of lime and charcoal. Then they put the beads into a revolving barrel partly filled with sand and set the barrel in the lehr. The hot fire hardened the beads, and the tumbling action in the sand rounded the sharp edges made by the guillotine. The mixture of lime and charcoal kept the hole of the bead from collapsing from the heat. For a high polish, the beads were sifted from the sand and placed in a sack of bran and shaken vigorously. Using the draw method, beadmakers could make large numbers of fairly uniform beads. Most often they made single-color cylinder beads, called bugles, or small seed beads. Some people called the small round beads tumbled beads. Merchants who bought them wholesale by weight called them pound beads.

The most skilled craftsmen also made chevron, or star, beads. Peoples as far apart as the Yoruba in Nigeria and the Crow Indians in Montana cherished chevrons. To make one, the beadmaker built up a cylinder of three major colors, each separated from the next by a thin layer of white. When the cylinder was complete, the master beadmaker heated it up one last time and a runner drew it. After the canes were cut into bead-size lengths of two centimeters, the beadmakers ground flat planes, or facets, into the ends of the large bead. This exposed the different layers of color. The white layer outlined each plane and gave the appearance of a twelve-pointed star.

Wire-winding was the other method of making beads. Because the process did not require a large furnace, this technique was done in Venice proper. Unlike drawn beads that were cut from a long glass cane and were nearly identical, wire-wound beads were made one by one.

The beadmakers started with a cane of glass made on Murano by the draw method but without the hole. Over a hot burner the beadmaker softened the cane enough to wrap the end around a chalked wire. He made four or five at a time, using the flame to make them perfectly round. Using as many canes as he liked, a beadmaker built layer upon layer of glass. In this way he could make a very large bead of many colors. After making a large bead, he could reheat it until it was soft and press into it pieces of colored glass. Wire-winding was slower than drawing beads, but it could be done in small shops with simple equipment.

The pride of the beadmakers of Murano and Venice was the millefiori, or thousand-flower, bead, originated by the Egyptians but forgotten in Roman and medieval times. Starting with a gather of transparent glass, the worker shaped it into a cylinder and then dipped it into three or four different colors of glass. The beadmaker lowered the multilayered cylinder into a form whose inner walls were lined with canes of another color, often milky white. When the entire mass was heated in the reheating furnace, the beadmaker twisted the cylinder to make a complicated pattern. Then it was reheated a final time and drawn by a runner.

When this multilayered cane hardened, an assistant cut it into very thin disks, each a cross section of the complicated color pattern of the multilayered cylinder. The master beadmakers reheated the disks and pressed them into large wire-wound beads. By making millefiori beads in two steps—the first, making the elaborate cane that was cut into disks; the second, adding the disks to a wire-wound bead—the beadmaker produced true works of art. Flowers, honeycombs, and stars were the most popular patterns.

After the beads were formed, they were put into sacks and delivered to stringers. These were women who sat along the streets of Murano and Venice putting the beads on long needles with strings attached. A skilled stringer held eight to ten needles in each

● A string of millefiori beads made in Venice in the nineteenth century.

hand. On each needle she picked up twenty-five beads and then let them slide down the string. She then tied the long strings and hung them from poles that were delivered to the warehouse. Some people came to buy in Venice, but most of the beads went to large wholesale operations in Amsterdam, London, Paris, and Cairo. Bead salesmen sailed all over the world carrying samples or pattern books of drawings of the different sorts of beads for sale back in Venice.

The samples or design patterns were arranged by type of bead, color, and size. A buyer could select from over five hundred categories of beads. Retailers bought the simpler, drawn beads by weight. More elaborate beads such as millefiori and chevrons were sold by the bunch or string.

Around 1600, 251 bead furnaces were working on Murano, and 100 beadmakers were making wire-wound beads in Venice. Throughout the seventeenth and eighteenth centuries, the industry produced between 500 and 800 pounds of beads a day, between 175,000 and 280,000 pounds per year. After Napoleon conquered Venice, bead production fell off. But by 1850 demand for beads to trade with the Indians in the American West revived the bead industry.

About 1900, the glass industry introduced new fuels and mechanical processes that greatly increased output. Beautiful wire-wound glass beads are still made all over the world in small factories, but the mass production of beads is mostly in Czechoslovakia and Japan. In place of the Venetian runners and guillotines, machines draw the glass canes, cut them into small segments, and tumble them in large drums in gas-fueled furnaces. Beadmakers are still secretive about their formulas for glass and the compounds for certain colors. Today as in the past, more elaborate beads require hand labor and are individual works of art.

BEADS AS
MONEY, BEADS
AS DOCUMENTS

2 People in Africa, the South Sea islands, and America have until modern times used beads as money. Before Christopher Columbus set out to find a short route to India, he knew that explorers of Africa took glass beads to trade with Africans for food, water, and slaves. Columbus did likewise. Upon landing on San Salvador Island, he gave the natives strings of glass beads.

Before the arrival of Europeans, American Indians made beads of stone, seeds, animal and fish bones, and shells. But glass they had never seen. After Columbus, Cortéz offered the Aztec Indians of Mexico glass beads in return for gold. Montezuma, the Aztec chief, accepted the trade, hoping that the Spaniards would be satisfied and leave them in peace. But the sight of gold brought the white men to stay—and to conquer.

In 1549, the Spanish fortune seeker Coronado and a small band of conquistadors marched north from Mexico into what is now New Mexico and Arizona in search of the fabled seven cities of gold. They failed to find the cities but they left in their trail through the southwest thousands of glass trade beads. Most of these were made on Murano.

The beadmakers of Murano also made translucent bugle beads with many facets, which were carried to China by English trading

13

companies. The beads, mostly blue, green, or amber, were traded to the Russians, who brought them to northwest America to exchange for furs. Many of these beads reached the southwest, where the Indians and whites called them Russians.

Colonists on the east coast of North America also brought glass beads to trade with the Indians. The settlers in Jamestown, Virginia, hired glassmakers from Murano to set up a bead factory in 1622, but Indians destroyed the colony that year. Afterward settlers in the New World depended on glass beads imported from Murano and, later, Bohemia in central Europe. To the north, Dutch and English colonists found that the coastal Indians used shell beads as adornment and sometimes as money. The Montauk Indian name for these beads was *wampumpeag*, meaning white (*wamp*) stringing beads (*umpeag*). The Europeans called them wampum.

To make wampum, Indians gathered whelk shells shaped like conches from the shallow waters of the Atlantic. The Indian worker, usually a woman, chipped off everything from the central whorl, then ground it into a slender column five or six inches long. With a piece of sandstone, she cut the column into quarter-inch lengths. Using a sliver of flint or slate, she then laboriously drilled a hole the length of the shell segment.

Because they made or grew almost everything they needed and did not trade with one another a great deal, Indians used wampum as currency only on occasion. But they did use wampum to settle disputes and to pay penalties for disobeying tribal law. For example, if one member of a tribe injured another in a fight or by accident, the first would pay the second so much wampum. In this way, wampum prevented feuds from breaking out. The value of wampum remained stable because it was very hard to make and because workers kept the quality high. Indians considered wampum sacred. It was unthinkable to make a rough or inadequately drilled bead.

In the 1600s, Dutch traders upset the traditional balance of supply and demand of wampum. In Holland, beaver hats with broad brims were in fashion. Every burgher and lady of standing had to have a beaver hat, and demand for beaver among the prosperous Dutch became insatiable. To sell beaver pelts to the Dutch, the coastal Indians demanded wampum. They showed little interest in gold or silver. Glass beads were all right for decoration and some trade, but in exchange for beaver, Indians required shell beads.

Needing a large supply of wampum, the Dutch, and later the English, set up small wampum factories near their trading posts. They hired Indians to make the wampum that Dutch traders would then give to the tribes for beaver pelts. To improve the manufacture of wampum, the Dutch gave the Indians metal drills and awls to make quicker and better bores.

The introduction of metal tools revolutionized wampum-making, not only by making production faster but also by enabling the In-

● In the early 1800s, white settlers took over the making of wampum from the Indians. A New Jersey workshop used this drilling machine to make several beads at once.

dians to make beads from the quahog, a hard-shelled clam. Near the hinge that joined the quahog's two parts, or valves, the shell is purple. In young quahogs the purple is just a tint, but in older clams found in deeper water the shell has a large patch of purple. Because the purple shell was harder to find than the white, beads of this color—which the Indians called black—were more valuable than the common white. Using metal drills, the Indians learned how to make beautiful purple wampum.

The worker first knocked away the white part, leaving the purple part of the clam valve. This was ground on a stone covered with sand until it was a little bigger than its final size of a quarter of an inch deep by an eighth of an inch in diameter. To drill the hole, a metal drill was fixed in the end of a foot-long shaft. Around the shaft was looped the string of a short bow. Holding the end of the shaft either in her hand with a crosspiece or against her chest on a metal plate, the worker pulled the bow back and forth, making the shaft turn. Every few turns, she took the drill out of the shell, cleaned it off, and cooled it with a few drops of water. Drilling proceeded slowly lest the drill become too hot and shatter the brittle shell. After the hole was bored, the worker polished. When oiled with a little animal fat, the shell bead shone like a jewel. So finely was wampum finished and polished that early French explorers called it porcelain. A skilled worker could make about eight strings a day, each string ten inches long and holding fifteen to twenty beads.

The Dutch regulated the worth of wampum according to "one finished beaver"—that is, a skin ready to go to the tanner. Mostly wampum was measured by the fathom, the span from fingertips to fingertips of a man's outstretched arms. Arm spans vary, so the fathom was fixed at 180 purple beads and twice as many white. In general, purple wampum was worth twice as much as white. At one point in the early 1600s, the Dutch flooded the market with wampum. This excess inflated the price of pelts. But as long as beaver remained plentiful, the price in wampum stayed fairly stable.

Unfortunately, Dutch greed for beaver fed the Indian greed for wampum. For their own needs, Indians had killed only a few animals in a beaver house, leaving the rest to multiply. But the Dutch market blinded the Indians to the wisdom of their ancestors. They killed all the beaver they could find and traded them for wampum. As the beaver supply diminished, the price per pelt rose. By the late 1600s, coastal Indians had destroyed their beaver population, and traders from many countries pushed inland.

From 1620 to 1660 wampum was also the official currency among the white settlers. Coin money was scarce, and much of the business of the settlers depended on things supplied by the Indians. While sacred to the Indians, wampum proved practical for the whites. The English colonies set the price at so many beads per penny. White people paid for pots and pans, seeds, and canoes, all with wampum. Harvard College accepted part of its tuition fee in the white and purple beads.

Even after the beaver were killed off and wampum was no longer an official currency, colonists continued to use wampum as small change. In 1693 the ferry from Manhattan to Brooklyn cost sixty white or thirty purple wampum. All through the 1700s and into the early 1800s the citizens of Bergen County, New Jersey, carried and accepted wampum for purchases at general stores.

By 1700, the Dutch had been pushed out by the English. New Amsterdam was renamed New York. The beaver boom collapsed, but wampum was in greater demand than ever—not on the coast, but inland in the interior of New York State.

In the mid-1500s, the famous Iroquois chief Hiawatha had brought together the Mohawk, the Seneca, the Cayuga, the Oneida, and the Onondaga (all spoke the Iroquois language) into the league of Five Nations. According to Iroquois legend, the chiefs of the tribes buried their hatchets in the roots of a large pine tree, made five strings of white wampum, and tied them together to show their union. Whenever the chiefs met to discuss a problem, they took out the five strings and recalled their pledge to work together. The simple wampum strings reminded the chiefs of their strength in

● Wampum belts woven and presented by northeast American Indians to seal treaties.

unity, helping the Five Nations to live in peace with one another for a hundred years.

Banded together, the Iroquois league took over New York State from the other tribes in the 1600s. The Iroquois used white and purple wampum beads to seal agreements and treaties and to record important events. The combination of white and purple wampum made it possible for the Iroquois to weave designs that gave the meaning of a treaty or event in abstract form. In general, white stood for peace, happiness, prosperity; purple for trouble, hardship, or something weighty. But it was the combination that mattered. The powerful Iroquois league conquered many tribes to the west and south. Everywhere they warred or traded they brought declarations of war, offers of peace, and other messages woven in patterns of white and purple wampum. When an Iroquois messenger arrived at the council of another tribe, he lay (the Indians said threw) the wampum message at the feet of the tribal leaders. Wampum became so important as a diplomatic communication that a tribe would not welcome a messenger from another tribe unless he carried a wampum belt or wampum string.

In their dealings with William Penn, around 1680, the Delaware Indians to the south of the Iroquois made and threw several belts. The Freedom Belt shows a path of white moving up and down across the belt. These lines reminded Penn and his fellow Quakers that, though the Delaware had sold the land to the colonists, the Indians kept the right to hunt, fish, and pass through the territory. In accepting the belt, Penn agreed to these terms. Another belt shows the four tracts of land Penn purchased, and a third pictures two figures holding hands. The belts Penn accepted from the Delaware were typical wampum records of treaties. The belts were unusual in that during William Penn's lifetime, the colonists abided by the terms.

As white men pushed farther into the interior of North America, wampum came into greater and greater use, both as currency and as message material. Along with fancy trade beads and seed beads, wampum went from white men's hands into Indian pouches as payment for land, furs, and services. Although most white settlers

● The Freedom Belt given by the Delaware Indians to William Penn. The meandering design shows the right of the Indians to cross land after they had sold it to Penn.

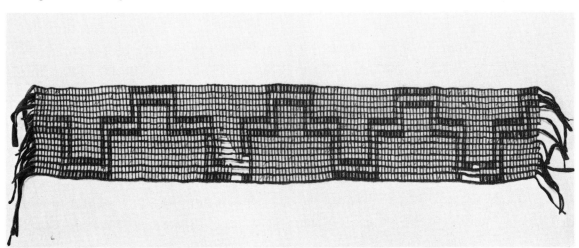

simply drove the earliest inhabitants of America from their homelands, some paid for it and tried to ensure fair treatment of the Indians. One such man was William Penn. Another, William Johnson, not only paid for his land but took up Indian ways. He married a Mohawk princess and kept his estate in upper New York open to Indian friends. Whenever the Indians and white men started to fight, Johnson, who was Superintendent of Indian Affairs, would hold a large council to which everyone was invited. Indians and settlers ate together and then made peace treaties. Johnson provided barrels of wampum, and, as agreements were reached, the Indian women quickly wove wampum belts. Although the settlers often broke the agreements, the Indians respected Johnson and his knowledge of their ways. When the Superintendent of Indian Affairs died, Indians from all over came and covered his body with wampum strings and belts.

Strangely enough, in the 1700s, the manufacture of wampum passed into white men's hands. As the Indians were defeated and pushed out of their native lands, settlers took over factories on Long Island and New Jersey. The Campbell shop in Pascack, New Jersey, was the most famous and remained in business until the early 1900s. John Campbell started production in 1735. He supplied big users like William Johnson and important Iroquois chiefs. Business flourished. During the American Revolution, the Campbell shop sold wampum to Washington's army for their dealings with Indians. After the Revolution, the Campbells sold beads to trading companies. In 1802, the North West Company bought 200,000 white and purple beads to use to buy furs in the northwest.

As long as there was frontier to conquer, the wampum business prospered. By the 1880s, the great herds of buffalo had given way to towns and railroads. From the Indans, white men had bought or taken—mostly taken—everything of value. The Indians themselves were forced to live on reservations. Wampum lost its usefulness, and in 1905, after 170 years of business, the Campbell shop closed its doors forever.

AFRICAN TRADE-WIND BEADS

3 As far back as 150 B.C., Arabs navigated the sea routes connecting India, the Persian Gulf, and East Africa. After the rise of Islam in the 600s, the caliphs ruled such a large and prosperous empire that Arab ships dominated trade along a vast coastal rim that stretched from Djakarta, Indonesia, to Dar es Salaam, Tanzania. The Arab sailing ships, called dhows, looked like small Spanish galleons and ranged in size from twenty to several hundred feet long. They were double-ended, coming to a point at both bow and stern. The timbers of the hull were teak or coconut, oily woods that resisted the ocean's salt and glistened in the tropical sun.

Caliphs, merchants, shopkeepers, and others who benefited from the riches of the Islamic empire called the winds that swept westward across the Indian Ocean from October to April trade winds because they brought silk, jewels, ivory, spices, and exotic stories to Middle Eastern bazaars and homes. During the summer months, winds from the southwest carried dhows up the coast of East Africa to Red Sea and Persian Gulf ports, where goods were transferred to caravans bound for Cairo, Damascus, Medina, and other large cities. Since the winds from the southwest blew less predictably than the trade winds from the east, Arab ships sailing the East African route often had to hug the coast, using a flitting movement called ghosting.

The eastward journey from Africa, against prevailing winds, was always more difficult than the westward journey.

Dangers of the trip in any season included pirates, island reefs, and sudden storms. Sailors called the waves off the African coast mountain waves or blind waves. Their crests had no white caps to warn captains of the vast peaks and valleys that lay ahead.

Arab sailors loved to tell stories about Sindbad, the clever sea merchant of *The Arabian Nights' Entertainment*. In one story Sindbad travels to India, where he acquires a load of coconuts by throwing stones at monkeys perched in coconut palms. The monkeys return fire with fresh coconuts. Sindbad then uses the coconuts to hire natives to dive for pearls for bead necklaces, which he later sells on his return to Baghdad.

Sindbad also traveled to East Africa. In the markets there the currency was beads. Since most of these beads came from India, they were called trade-wind beads. In order to do business along the East African coast, Arab sea captains loaded their vessels with barrels of beads made in northern India. These were wire-wound and drawn-glass beads—most popularly red but also green, blue, and yellow—semiprecious stone beads such as carnelian, agate, and quartz, and metal beads. Arab merchants traded these beads for ivory, gold, ambergris, tortoise shell, coffee, spices, and slaves. Although the Africans made some of their own beads for adornment and magic, all their trading beads came from abroad.

Most ships arriving from India and the Near East docked first at the big, wide harbor of Zanzibar, the island off present-day Tanzania. Zanzibar, with its many shade trees and abundant fresh water, was a welcome sight to the sailors. Trade in its marketplace was brisk. There sea merchants who were unwilling to sail all the way to India could stock up on beads from wholesale suppliers.

In the 1500s the Portuguese wrested control of the sea routes from the Arabs. Portuguese traders seemed always short of beads. Vasco da Gama, the famous navigator, put in at East African ports with European beads in unfashionable colors and shapes. He had to

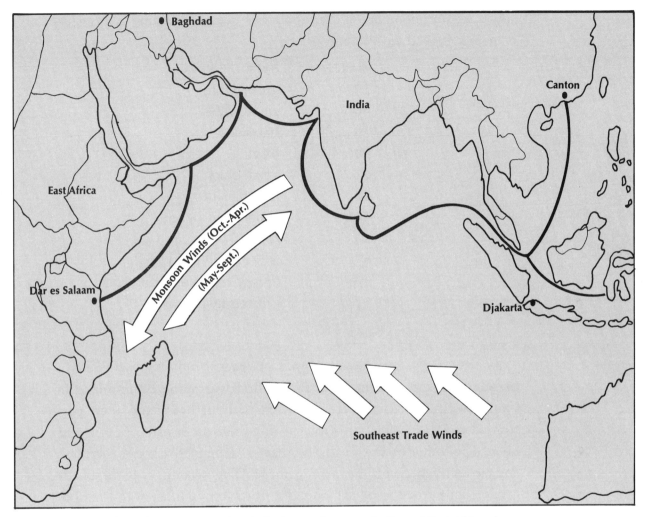

● Map of the Indian Ocean trade winds. Arrows between India and East Africa show seasonal monsoon winds. Arrows from the southeast represent winds that blow off and on all year long.

sail to India to pick up acceptable beads. On the way he lost a ship. Similarly, Jan van Riebeeck, who founded the Dutch colony at the Cape of Good Hope in 1651, had to have brass beads shipped over from Java when the native Hottentots refused Venetian beads as barter.

In 1680, on a trading mission to East Africa, the English ship *Mary* carried fifty barrels of cowrie shells and eleven chests of beads. The ship's account book listed the number of beads according to bunches or packs. It read as follows:

BUNCHES	TYPE OF BEAD
121	great white
66	small white
78	hair color
94	black
61	small black
62	lemon color
112	lemon transparent
52	red
67	white
57	orange transparent
113	green transparent
total 883	

By the 1800s, two general types of trade beads were current in the marketplaces of East Africa. The first was stone beads made in Cambray, India. They were imported without holes and then perforated in Africa. Merchants then strung them on threads of palm-leaf fiber. The value of the beads for barter depended on the evenness and attractiveness of the arrangement. The second type of beads came from Europe, especially Venice, the Netherlands, and, later on, Czechoslovakia. Most prized of the European beads were the millefiori from Venice.

In 1852 the English explorer Sir Richard Burton arrived in Zanzibar. Before he could venture inland, he had to wait for a shipment of beads from Venice. While waiting for this currency to come, he got together a large supply of Indian beads in the local markets. Although Burton learned the marketplace language of Swahili in a mere month and had mastered dozens of other languages, he too had a hard time staying current with styles of beads. He had to throw out a large sack of cheap black-and-white beads because the Africans considered them worthless, not even proper as a gift.

Burton also found that the value of certain types of beads varied greatly from one market town to another. In one marketplace the light-blue "pigeon eggs" fetched more goods than did little pink porcelain round beads. In another marketplace the opposite was true. Cheaper varieties of beads would purchase grain and vegetables, but not fowl, milk, and eggs. "Learn the prices of all beads in a strange village before entering it," Burton advised.

As he traveled inland, Burton used his beads as gifts to local chieftains. The explorer's caravan carried a red flag informing villagers that they were peaceful traders and not slavers. After the caravan entered a village, presents were exchanged. The chieftain gave a gift of a goat and a calabash of meal to the leader of the safari. Burton offered beads in return. If the headman was unfamiliar with the beads, he would consult with his comrades before taking them. Feasting and dancing rounded out the evening.

At a campsite near Lake Ziwa, Ethiopia, Burton came face to face with the powerful chief of the Pogoro. The old man held himself very straight and spoke in a tone of great authority. He was dressed in a loincloth and sandals, and his torso was shiny with oil. Strings loaded with beads decorated his neck.

The explorer, crisply dressed in white shirt and trousers, and the African chief carefully eyed each other. The chief demanded a fee for traveling across his land. Burton took this as an insult and ordered his weary helpers to break camp and move elsewhere. As forcing the travelers to leave his territory would violate the law of hospitality, the chief quickly entreated Burton to stay as his guest. Burton agreed and presented the proud leader with two long pieces of cloth and a few strings of cigar-shaped red glass beads to add to the chief's collection. "Better this slight spending than the chance of a flight of arrows during the night," Burton wrote in his travel diary that evening.

Along the coast of Africa beads were used as small change, but inland they were the most important currency. A traveler had to be careful to spend his beads slowly. Imagine going on a long trip and

● Various trade-wind beads used as currency in East Africa.

taking all of your cash in half-dollars. The most a man could carry in a sack on his shoulder was a load of fifty pounds of beads, good for only a month of purchases in Burton's time. Without bearers to carry a large supply of beads, a foreigner traveling into the interior of East Africa would have to turn back after a few weeks. For a trial trip of a few weeks down the African coast, Burton carried thirty-five pounds of small white and pink Venetian beads. His hired hands carried them in long bags slung between poles.

Here are some food prices Burton noted at a rather expensive market in Kwale, Kenya, in April 1858: a strand of orange beads as long as twice the circumference of the throat, called a *khete* length, bought a hen or fifty cucumbers or three cups of milk. Large fish cost two *khete*. Firewood, which had to be brought in canoes from considerable distances, was expensive, a *khete* being the price of a little bundle of seventy-five sticks. Most in fashion was the large blue glass bead. One *khete* of this kind, equal to three of the orange, would buy a pound of cotton.

Each kind of trade bead had three or four different names in East African dialects. Red-on-white enameled beads were known as scarlet cloth. Because a person would go without dinner to obtain them, they were also called food finishers. Because some women would bankrupt their families for them, they were also named town breakers. The children's favorites were white porcelain beads. They were used for playing games like *oware*, decorating dolls, and for personal adornment. Some beads like the so-called king's bead, a brown bead the size of a shooter marble and with painted stripes, passed hands when a lavish gift was needed. Until recently in Zambia, a single king's bead could pay for a cow or hire a boat for a long journey.

BEAD
MESSAGES

4 The Zulus of South Africa love beadwork. They wear beads as ornaments and for communication. The kinds of bead, their colors, and the pattern of the weave may tell a person's position in the community, whether married or dating, an important emotion, and even a past event. Among Zulu teen-agers, bead ornaments are badges of courtship and love.

Zulus begin wearing beads a few days after they are born. While babies nurse, mothers string simple anklets and bracelets for them. As they grow up, Zulu children learn everything about beads. Boys help bargain for beads at the local store. Girls are taught how to cover mirrors, pipes, whistles, bottles, and tin cans with colorful beads. They learn to decorate aprons, shawls, skirts, blankets, bags, and even umbrellas in bead patterns specially designed for important occasions. All of this prepares young people for the romance of love-letter badges later on.

Zulus live in small, circular compounds called kraals, a word like our word "corral." Each family occupies a small hut. Unmarried boys and unmarried girls form groups that are as influential as the family. For example, when a girl has her first period, she stays indoors until it is over. But all the unmarried girls and boys of the kraal gather outside her hut every night to dance and sing. The drum they play is called the menstruation drum. The songs they sing are about romantic love. In this way, it is the young people of the kraal who usher a girl into womanhood.

After the celebration, the girl lets her hair grow long and decorates it with beautiful beads. This tells everybody in the village that she is eligible for marriage. Whenever she goes to the river to fetch water or to the store to buy cloth, young men flirt with her and try to win her favor. If a youth takes a fancy to an eligible girl, he will do extravagant things to show his affection. He puts plumes in his hair, bells on his ankles, and finds excuses to hang around the girl's hut. If a girl wants to encourage a boy, she makes him bead jewelry. The most popular girls enjoy a lot of attention as they walk about the kraal, and the most popular boys wear many strands of beads. Every girl attracts at least one suitor, and every boy wears at least one strand of beads. In this way the boys and girls get acquainted with the other unmarried youth of the village and have a choice for their permanent mate.

Bead messages are most often worked into neck ornaments. The *ibheqe* (pronounced i-bee-kwa) is the most common sort. This small necklace consists of a narrow beaded band long enough to encircle the neck, fastened by a two-looped thread buttonhole and large round egg-shaped beads, which serve as buttons. Attached to the band so it hangs over the hollow of the throat is a square patch, or flap, of beadwork. Sometimes several flaps are placed one on top of another like the pages of a book.

A girl makes a pair of *ibheqes*. She gives one to a boy who attracts her, the other she keeps and wears. They are especially popular as gifts to boy friends who have moved to the cities of South Africa, like Durban, to earn enough cash to get married. The *ibheqe* serves as a memento reminding the boy far from his village of the lovely girl back home.

The *ibheqe* is an informal link and doesn't mean the two are going steady. The boy is still free to date other girls and the girl has

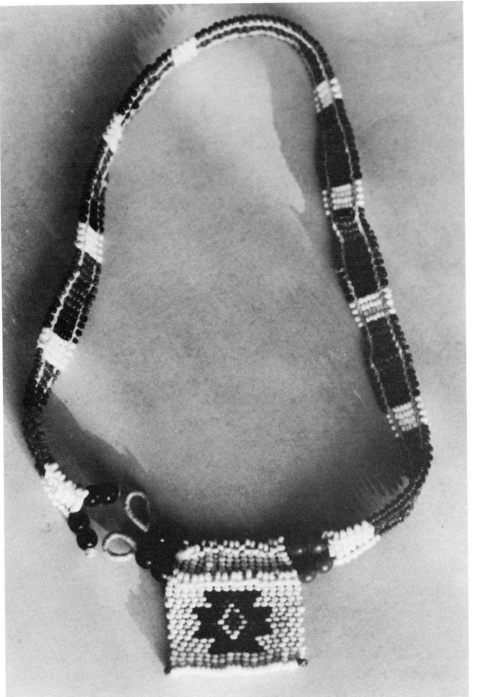

● An *ibheqe* belonging to a Zulu girl in KwaZulu, South Africa.

expressed only an interest. The number of *ibheqes* a boy wears shows a girl how much competition she has. When she sees him wearing a whole stack of them, she may press for an early formal engagement. This is the occasion for a big outdoor party, generally in a wooded area, with friends the same age serving as witnesses. At the party the girl hands the boy a necklace of white beads five yards long. Called an *ucu*, it serves the same purpose as our engagement ring. The young man wears this as a necklace only on the day his fiancée accepts him. Afterward he returns it to the girl, who then doubles and twists it to form a kind of braid. This short version of the *ucu* announces the couple's bond in marriage. After giving the *ucu*, the girl makes similar bead strips for her waist, wrist, and ankles. As soon as she wears them she is called a young woman and is permitted to wear more lavish bead ornaments and to beautify herself with cosmetics and high hair styles.

Some of the *ibheqes* are letters in which the colors and patterns of the beads declare love, seek engagement, or even express disappointment. If a boy finds it hard to interpret a message, he asks his sisters to help him. All the girls are clever at deciphering because they weave beads among groups of friends.

The system is based on color-coding. Colors represent words and combinations represent ideas. In reading a message, a Zulu boy takes note of three things: the color of the beads, their position in the overall pattern, and the background. The main colors of beads in love messages are white, red, blue, green, yellow, pink, and black. Each color represents a special thing and has a number of meanings —including at least one favorable and one unfavorable. The only exception is white, which contrasts well with dark skin and stands for everything good. Zulus compare white beads to the purity of sand and call them sea sand.

The names of the bead colors come from things in nature having those colors. For example, a green bead with stripe is called a grasshopper. A list of the most popular beads with some of their names and possible interpretations follows:

White	bones = happiness, purity, good luck, love, children
Red (opaque)	blood = strong emotion; tears
Red (transparent)	fire = a burning heart, intense longing; or anger, impatience
Yellow	pumpkin = a garden, a household, diligence, wealth; or thirst, withering, baldness
Green	new grass = contentment; or sickness, an argument
Pink	= a promise, high rank, or high birth; or poverty, laziness
Black	a kaross (a Zulu bridal skirt made of black animal hide) = marriage; or darkness, disappointment, misfortune
Royal blue	mountain dove = faithfulness, a request; or ill feeling
Navy blue	= news; or gossip

The double and triple meanings a bead message may have make them tricky to translate. The different meanings of one color are like the different meanings we can give to a word by shifting our tone of voice. "Great" said in a happy, excited way is high praise. But push the word low in your throat, drawling it flatly—"greaat"—and the word won't sound like a compliment any more. Far from it. It sounds as if you had said, "Terrible." "Great" can express two contrary feelings. So can two blue beads. To understand which is which you must know the meaning of the "sentence" or "paragraph" of beadwork into which they are woven.

Colors against a white background signify the favorable choice of a meaning. Blue, white, and black in combination bring to any design many joyous meanings. Those colors together suggest a wedding. Two other color schemes are frequently used. One has green dominating, while in the other red and yellow form the main colors. Both color schemes use white, blue, and black beads.

Weaving in colors that don't suit one another gives an unfavorable meaning. Certain colors don't "belong" in either the green or red-yellow schemes. In Zulu eyes, yellow clashes with green. Red and green seldom go together. Pinks are out of place in a red-yellow design. Expressing rejection, dislike, or disappointment is strongest when opposing colors such as green and yellow lie side by side. Including them in the same design but separated by other colors indicates mild reproach or mixed feelings.

Just as a boy proudly wears messages of affection, so also must he wear a necklace that says he was jilted. Such a rejection is usually all black beads and certainly no white ones. As in teen-age romance everywhere, a black *ibheqe* is not the end of the world. In the end most Zulu boys and girls find a mate.

Another key to reading a bead message is design. Where a girl places certain colors within a pattern is important. Squares, triangles, and diamonds are the most popular geometries. A girl weaves the shapes according to her imagination, but she is careful about the sequence of different color beads.

For example, she may arrange a single bead in one color and pairs of beads in other colors at either side of the center bead. The single bead in the middle is the point at which the order is reversed. The meaning is then read from one edge to the other, ending at the center. In a bead message that has the sequence red bead, yellow, blue, yellow, red, here is the interpretation. Because it starts and ends the message, red stands for anger. Yellow on either side of blue suggests wilting or pining away, like the dying leaves of a neglected garden. The color at the turning point, blue, stands for a request, indicating that the giver asks a question and expects a reply. The whole message goes as follows: I am angry. You are neglecting me. When will you return?

A few beads of a contrasting color can be used to punctuate the series, marking it off from the rest of the beadwork on the ornament. For this a color that otherwise might be considered a clash can be used. Because the rules for these patterns are part of custom, they are used only when the sender lives nearby the receiver.

A last key is intensity of color. Extra beads in the same color lay stress on a meaning. Expressing a feeling with a very few beads and then overshadowing it with another color can soften the message. In the message just described, more red beads than yellow would suggest great anger. Adding yellow and reducing reds would change the anger to displeasure. The presence of even one white bead can change a negative meaning to some or a little anger.

White can also be used to shade the message. By using pink next to red, a girl says, "You are poor," but if she adds white next to the pink, she changes the message by adding "but I love you."

All these messages are public, just like the classified ads in our newspapers that declare, "Jerry, I miss you. Come home," or "Happy birthday, sweetheart." Everyone who speaks the language of colors can figure them out. It is also possible, though, for a girl to keep a bead message more private. Just as we might put something in a locket, she may so cleverly hide a single pink bead among a large patch of white ones that it is almost invisible. You might even think it was a mistake when in fact it is a bit of information, probably referring to a promise that has been made, or maybe to the fact that the lover is from an important family.

A succession of many white, red, green, blue, black and white beads would be interpreted this way:

> *My heart is pure in the long days.*
> *My eyes are sore from looking for you for so long.*
> *I have grown lean and sickly.*
> *If I were a dove I would fly to your home.*
> *Darkness prevents my coming to you.*
> *But my heart is pure.*

WEST AFRICAN BEADS

5 Zulu beads tell the most, but there is hardly a people or village in Africa that does not wear or use beads in a distinctive way. The people of West Africa make beads from many different substances and objects—animal teeth and claws, roots, nuts that rattle, cowrie shells, and glass.

The oldest West African beads are stone. Because beadmakers used bowdrills, the holes in old stone beads are crooked. With a primitive bowdrill, a beadmaker drilled first from one end, then from the other. This method prevented the valuable stone from shattering. One West African town, Ilorin, Nigeria, still has professional stone-beaders. These men and women make beads from red jasper that is brought down on barges from quarries in Upper Volta. The jasper is chipped, chiseled, and pierced with hand tools. To do the piercing, the beadmaker holds the stone between his or her toes and punches it with a sharp-edged hammer coated with palm oil. Nigerians use stone beads like these jasper ones to replace missing beads in heirloom headdresses and garments.

Africans living in the Gold Coast, in the bulge of West Africa, value their aggry beads as much as gold. The name aggry comes from a word for a blue coral that grows in bushes on the bottom of rivers and lakes in Benin. Beginning in the sixteenth century, Euro-

37

peans brought the coral south from Benin to markets where they bartered it for copper bracelets and supplies. There aggry was cut and shaped into smooth beads for necklaces and hair ornaments.

In the language Africans invented to talk with European dealers, "aggry" came to have another meaning: multicolored chevron trade beads. Like the millefiori bead described in Chapter 1, this aggry is built up of colored canes of glass into the shape of a barrel. The large bead is hacked along a diagonal slant at both ends before the glass hardens. The cuts near the hole expose the different layers of the glass. The colored canes are highest at the hole through the bead and lowest on the outside surface, making a squiggly pattern of colored V-shaped stripes, or chevrons. Aggries are up to two inches long and quite heavy.

Striped aggries were originally made on Murano specifically for export to Africa. Berber camel caravans transported these trade beads across the Sahara Desert to Timbuktu and other trading

● Chevron beads made in Venice. In West Africa, these are called aggries.

towns. Today the glass beads are made in Japan and Czechoslo-vakia as well as in Venice. They come into Africa through Morocco.

The value of an aggry depends as much on its past as on its beauty. The people of Benin and neighboring countries believe the beads carry the spirit or personality of former owners. If the person who used to wear the beads was highly esteemed or of royalty, the person's stature has rubbed off onto the beads. In this way, aggry beads are like diamond rings in our culture, which we cherish for more than their resale value.

Since wearers of aggry beads prefer old ones, they apply two tests. First they look for an opening that is uneven from many years of being worn on a string. Second, they want a sheen that comes from constant wearing, weathering, and, they hope, burial in an ancestor's grave. Even the dark-colored chevron aggries light up like jewels in the sun because the inner layer of clear glass is visible near the hole.

In West Africa, only a chief can wear a string of chevron aggries. But many persons can afford one aggry strung alongside less costly beads on a bracelet or necklace. A bride receives an aggry from her family on her wedding day and passes it on as a precious heirloom to her granddaughter. Young men wear aggries on hairbands or armlets.

In traditional African religion, the earth that nurtures forests and crops and animals is held sacred. The energy of the soil has so impressed the people that they have long told stories of how the first human sprang from the earth like a plant. In Nigeria, an Ashanti legend tells that their ancestors once dwelt under the ground in caves. Part of this legend relates that when an Ashanti buried an aggry in the ground, it split into two aggries; if left undisturbed for generations, the aggry produced a whole "family" of aggries.

In Northern Ghana, Krobos make their own glass beads. The Krobo version of the glasshouse is a small mud hut with a pit in the center. In the pit is built a fire of dung, wood, and coal. To make the fire hot enough to melt the glass, the pit has two bellows

● A Nigerian beaded mask worn in religious dances.

built into its base. Each bellows is an animal stomach to which a stick is attached. A stick in each hand, a man pumps the bellows to the beat of a drummer, who sits alongside. Around the pit three or four glassmakers with long iron rods sit cross-legged.

Whereas the glassmakers of Murano melt silica in a crucible to make glass, Krobo craftsmen recycle glass bottles. At the end of an iron rod, a cobalt blue Phillips' Milk of Magnesia bottle slowly sags toward the fire. At just the right moment, the glassmaker catches a drip of molten glass with a second thin rod and rotates it to make a bead. To fashion it nicely round, he turns it over the fire. When the bead is formed, he taps the rod on the ground and the bead slides off. He then repeats the process by sticking the blue bottle back into the fire until another glob drips off.

As well as the blue medicine bottles, the beadmakers of Krobo love white cold-cream jars, amber beer bottles, and green soft-drink bottles. Using the wire-wound method, they build up beads of many colors and free designs. Krobo beads range in shape from thin disks to cylinders five centimeters long. They are sold in markets all over the continent.

Even though they lack hot fuel and brick furnaces, Nigeria's Ashanti people have also developed their own glass-bead industry. To the beat of an African drum, the Ashanti recycle used glass into new beads, turning the ordinary into beauty. In the craft center of Bida, the Ashanti make beads from glass powder they either import or make by grinding up old European glass beads. The beadmaker scoops up the powder with a snail shell. He taps an even layer into a mold and smooths it with a feather. More layers of different colors are added on top. Then he places the mold in a bed of burning charcoal. To raise the temperature further, a furnace is placed over the charcoal. The beadmaker fans the fire with a piece of animal hide or woven palm leaves. When the fire is hot enough, about four hundred degrees Fahrenheit, the glass powder melts. The result is a multicolored glass cane that the Ashanti craftsman pries from the mold, saws into short pieces, and bores with a bowdrill. To smooth a bead, the worker drives it into a piece of raw yam to hold the bead and grinds it against a stone slab.

Often West African beads have specific magical uses. Many Yoruba women in Nigeria give birth to twins. Anthropologists think that so many multiple births may come from eating a certain kind of yam. Yorubas themselves see twin births as a miracle and sign of fertility. Whether or not a family has twins, it usually owns *ibeji*, meaning twin statues, which it dresses gaily in beads and clothing and magic rings. The beads represent the fertile power of parents who conceive and give birth to twins. To share in this fertility, the owner of *ibeji* wears colored beads identical to those on the sculpture. A family's *ibeji* is especially important if, as often happens, one of a set of twins dies. The surviving twin keeps the *ibeji* close by for the rest of his or her life. Whenever the mother makes a new jacket or dress for the surviving twin, she also makes one for the *ibeji*. Just as the living twin needs larger and larger clothes, so does the mother make larger ones for the *ibeji*, putting the newest over the older clothes.

Beads in Africa also show political position. The Yoruba use tiny glass seed beads to cover a chief's throne, royal stool, and fly whisks. Some of the lavish objects bring bitter memories to Africans, because the chiefs acquired them by cooperating with slave traders. The Yoruba are also famous for their beaded crowns, which designate the right to rule. One Yoruba chief had forty of them!

Oduduwa, the first Yoruba king, had sixteen sons. He appointed them governors of sixteen states and gave each a beaded crown. Sixteen different species of birds decorated each crown. This reminded each prince that he shared authority with his fifteen brothers. Oduduwa also gave them other articles of clothing, including boots, each of which had four stuffed birds running up the front. Much later other chiefs claimed equal rank with Oduduwa's direct descendants. But their claims were rejected because their wardrobes lacked the beaded crowns and boots with birds.

● A Nigerian *ibeji* dressed in a cowrie shell robe.

DUTCH BEAD
GARDENS

6 The seventeenth century was the golden age of Holland. Dutch trading companies like the rich and powerful East India Company sent ships all over the world. Beads, along with mirrors, were the most important items they carried for trade. By 1600, a number of glassmakers had escaped from Venice or just migrated from other Italian cities to set up glass factories in the Netherlands. Six of these glasshouses made beads. We know that by 1613 one of these, in Amsterdam, employed eighty families. Even today you can find seventeenth-century Dutch beads in North and South America, Asia, and Africa.

During Holland's golden age, sea captains brought home from their voyages around the world chests full of odd lots of beads. Gradually the custom grew to decorate yards and gardens with these beads. Retired captains in particular took up the hobby of framing tulip beds, covering pathways, and lining garden pools with a great variety and quantity of beads. During the long, gray winters, while tulip bulbs lay dormant, old salts laid and restored colorful plots of beads.

In the 1700s, the English took away from the Dutch most of the trade with India. The East India Company's business fell off. Also, the Dutch glasshouses could not compete with the low prices of the other new bead-producing countries, Germany and Bohemia. As

● The star in the center of this Dutch garden is made of blue and white beads. The garden is located in the Netherlands Open Air Museum.

a consequence, a big stock of beads remained in the warehouses of Amsterdam.

With so many beads on hand, the sea captains' hobby of making bead gardens was taken up by other Netherlanders. Prosperous villagers in the area north of Amsterdam known as the Zaan region planted elaborate bead gardens. In the yards of their cheerfully painted wooden houses that faced a stream or canal, they laid out paths and geometric patterns of thousands of beads and shells.

The Dutch called these mineralogical gardens. They were composed of small make-believe caves and beds of colored beads. In the middle, the gardener kept plots of tulips and hyacinths, and perhaps a few trees. The Dutch read pattern books on how to make the gardens correctly. These books included sketches like

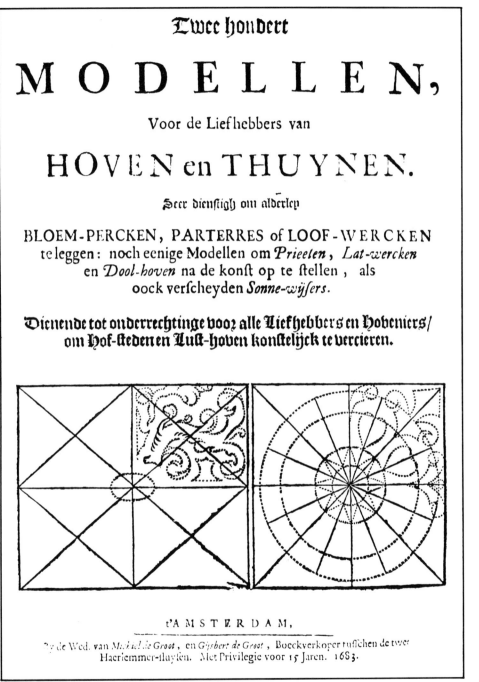

Twee hondert

MODELLEN,

Voor de Liefhebbers van

HOVEN en THUYNEN.

Seer dienstigh om alderley

BLOEM-PERCKEN, PARTERRES of LOOF-WERCKEN
te leggen : noch eenige Modellen om *Prieelen*, *Lat-wercken*
en *Dool-hoven* na de konst op te stellen, als
oock verscheyden *Sonne-wijsers*.

Dienende tot onderrechtinge voor alle Liefhebbers en Hoveniers/
om Hof-steden en Lust-hoven konstelijck te vercieren.

t'AMSTERDAM,

By de Wed. van *Michiel de Groot*, en *Gijsbert de Groot*, Boeckverkoper tusschen de twee
Haerlemmer-sluysen. Met Privilegie voor 15 Jaren. 1683.

● The title page from a book of garden designs popular in Holland in the seventeenth century. The title translates: "Two Hundred Patterns for Lovers of Tree Gardens and Flower Gardens."

knitting patterns, based on squares or circles. Large beads (six to ten millimeters long) in blue, brown, and milky white were most popular. Everything was exceptionally neat. Nowhere was a shell or bead out of place. The bead gardens were strictly off limits to dogs, geese, and ducks.

In the 1700s, the bead gardens of Zaandijk, a town in the Zaan region, were a favorite place to take a Sunday walk. Along the Zaan River stood dozens of wind-powered mills that ground flour, sawed lumber, pressed seed oil, and wove hemp rope. From the gardens lining the river, strollers had a splendid view of the rushing stream and windmills in one direction and the deep-green farmlands in the other direction.

Before the prosperous 1700s, Dutch families lived more simply, raising their own grain, grinding their own flour, baking their own bread. As trade began, these families often became burghers—that is, owners of small businesses. As the Dutch economy changed its emphasis from agriculture to manufacture and trade, the new middle class turned spaces that once were for grinding and bleaching the family's flour into bead gardens. In the middle of the area one or more small statues of stone, lead, or marble were placed on pedestals. This was the point around which were grouped flower beds or trees, under whose shade children played or adults escaped the summer heat.

The bead garden of the Honig family at Zaandijk was famous for a long time. It had beds inlaid with many colors of beads, in the middle of which rose a fake cave decorated with strange animals. With their glistening bead backs the beasts had a fantastical appearance in the sunshine.

During the early 1800s bead gardens fell out of fashion. Some were replanted while others, like the Honigs', fell into decay. In the eyes of new generations of tourists they were even grotesque. A nineteenth-century guidebook mentions the bead gardens this way: "Nor can the gardens bordering both sides of the road escape your attention. In former years they were embellished with boxwood,

● The "Statue Garden" in Zaandijk, Holland. A diamond-shaped plot of beads lies in the foreground.

shells, horns, multi-colored stones, and beads—truly colorful and in rather bad taste!"

The spread of the steam engine after 1850 gradually made Holland's graceful windmills obsolete. The once proud towers and their blades that made the wind do humans' work fell into disrepair and were torn down. But fortunately a few windmills were kept to remind the Dutch and others how Holland had once looked. Nor did the bead garden vanish altogether. About 1900, men repairing the canals of Zaandijk uncovered one of the old bead gardens. The citizens of Zaandijk restored the garden with new beads. The four corner beds now display the coats of arms of the Honig family and their ancestors. The rest of the plot features flower designs taken from a 1683 pattern book. This garden is one of the few survivors of the days when windmills beat before the sea winds and sea captains worked in their gardens with glass thumbs.

PRAYER
BEADS

7 Catholic and Orthodox Christians, Muslims, Hindus, and Buddhists all use rosaries to count prayers and meditations. In the Middle Ages, most Christians could not read the Bible or even understand the spoken Latin used in the Mass. So Irish monks taught them the Latin version of the Lord's Prayer found in Matthew 6:9–13. As a Christian started the Lord's Prayer with the words *Pater noster*, he or she slipped a berry or piece of wood or precious stone along a thread. In this way the earliest Christian prayer beads came to be known as a paternoster. Our word "patter," meaning speaking rapidly and without much thought, comes from paternoster. It carries the picture of those whose lips move fast and continuously as they tell their beads, often 150 at a sitting. Monks devoted to prayer and meditation were called paternosterers.

In the thirteenth century so many paternosterers were attached to St. Paul's Cathedral in London that making rosaries—turning, polishing, perforating, and stringing the beads—became a trade in itself. Four different guilds of craftsmen made them. Each guild worked in a different material. The first carved in bone and horn, the second in coral and mother-of-pearl, the third in amber and jet, while the fourth were metal workers who made buckles, rings, and buttons too.

In the late Middle Ages, more and more Christians said *Ave Maria*, or the prayer that begins "Hail Mary", instead of the Lord's Prayer. The name of the string of prayer beads shifted from paternoster to rosary. Originally, the Latin word *rosarium* meant an anthology or bouquet of choice passages from writings on a single subject, like law or philosophy. The Church extended this to mean a collection of prayers. As the custom of reciting 150 *Ave Marias*, or *Aves*, became more and more popular, the original identification of the prayer beads with the paternoster—Our Father—was laid aside. Eventually there was even an Ave Maria Lane in London.

In the sixteenth century a monk wrote a rosary picture book that gave illustrations of the fifteen most important events in the lives of Jesus and Mary. The idea was prayer with pictures. Each scene was enclosed in a garland of ten small roses and one big one. The big rose signified one Our Father said after every ten Hail Marys. The worshiper meditated on the first picture while saying the first ten *Aves*, turned to the next picture while saying the second ten, and so on. Taught by Dominican monks, picture books became so popular that all Catholics came to use the same form for the rosary prayers.

Because string wears away and breaks, almost all old rosaries have disappeared. However, there remain in museums spherical boxwood carvings that hung as pendants from the most lavish of all rosaries. These beads, about three inches in diameter, are intricately carved. The bead opens on a hinge and displays two hemispheres. In the hollow of each are carved scenes with a large number of tiny figures. Often a flat movable disk separates the two halves and is itself carved on both sides. Germans call them prayer nuts. They crop up as magical objects in fairy tales like the French story "The White Cat." The most magnificent boxwood bead was given on a rosary by King Henry VIII of England to a prominent cardinal. It is four inches across and has twenty-four different scenes carved inside. It is the ultimate wood bead, for it contains within it the history of the church that uses the bead to count its prayers.

● This sixteenth-century Flemish rosary bead, 2 ⁵/₈ in. in diameter, is made of boxwood.
The carved scenes on the inside show Christ leaving Jerusalem and the Crucifixion.

The Hindus of India were probably the first people to use prayer beads. Hindus believe that humans are destined to be reborn over and over. The cycle of death and rebirth holds in its grasp everybody except a few sages, who through study and meditation achieve liberation. For thousands of years these Hindu sages have concentrated on their prayers by holding a circlet of beads. The old Indian name for these beads is *mala*, meaning garden. A Hindu seeker hides the beads from sight when he says his *mala*. Sitting down, he either thrusts his right hand into a red bag resembling a big mitten or conceals it in the corner of a scarf wound around his body. With eyes closed he passes the beads between his thumb and middle finger, never using the index finger, which is unlucky. The hand is held close to the body while the beads are told—in the morning over the stomach, at noon on the heart, and in the evening close to the nose.

Each session with the beads is divided into three periods. If a man spends an hour over the *mala*, he tells his beads very loudly for the first twenty minutes, whispers slowly and quietly for the next twenty, and for the last twenty is so completely absorbed that he loses track of everything except the beads passing through his fingers.

Hindu prayer beads are often made from wood or seeds. Many Hindus love to tell stories of how the great god Vishnu from time to time descends to the world to defeat the forces of evil. The worshipers of Vishnu carry a rosary of 108 beads made of wood from the sacred tulasi tree. The number 108 comes from multiplying the twelve zodiac signs times nine (six visible planets plus the three stations of the moon—waxing, full, and waning). Every day the worshiper of Vishnu repeats the prayer 108 times, or three or five or ten times 108. The tulasi beads also play a part in the rite that brings children of seven or eight formally into the community. A string of 108 little beads is passed around their necks by the priest. He also teaches them a prayer word to use with the beads.

The devotees of Shiva, the god who created the universe by dancing, have prayer strings of thirty-four or sixty-four seeds of the rudraska tree. Called Shiva's tears, these seeds look like dark peach pits. Their rough surface is divided by grooves into five sections, which worshipers of Shiva regard as images of the five faces of the god. A legend says that one day Shiva cried in anger and his tears took the shape of the seeds.

Some Hindus say the bigger the beads, the more effective the prayers. About 1900 a traveler reported seeing a hermit who had in front of his hut a rosary of fifteen beads, each as large as a child's head and turned on a huge wooden roller.

About 500 B.C., Gautama Buddha simplified the Hindu quest for liberation by teaching the Middle Path. Buddha taught that compassion for all people and detachment from material things were the only ways to gain release from the cycle of birth, death, and rebirth. Buddha's simple teachings swept through India. After his death, Buddha's followers carried the teaching of the Middle Path southeast to Sri Lanka, Burma, and Thailand, and northeast to Tibet, China, and Japan. From the Hindus whom Buddha taught and converted, Buddhists borrowed prayer beads. Wherever the gentle message of the Middle Path traveled, prayer beads went along.

In Tibet nearly everybody carries prayer beads. Telling beads is still a steady habit for anybody whose work leaves the hands free. The Tibetan set contains 108 beads of equal size, like the Hindu one. It is made of jewels, sandalwood, or mussel shells, according to the owner's rank in society.

Attached to the beads is a pair of strings, each having ten small metal rings. One of the strings ends with a miniature *dorje,* a thunderbolt of Indra, the god who slays the dragons of darkness. The other ends with a small bell representing the Wheel of the Law. From *dorje* comes the name of the mountain town Darjeeling, where the famous black tea is grown.

The rings are counters too. Each ring in the *dorje* string stands for one circle of prayers. Each ring on the bell string marks tens of the circles. When about to tell the beads, the Tibetan slides the

● A Tibetan rosary. Tibetan monks use the metal rings on the four lower strands to count cycles of prayers.

counters up both strings. Once a round of beads is completed, he or she lets a counter slide down to touch the *dorje*. When all the ten counters are down (meaning that one hundred circles have been told), they are slid up again and one counter is slipped down the bell string. In this way the counters can register 108 x 10 x 10, or 10,800 prayers.

Early in his career, a Tibetan monk says 5,400 bead cycles a day. A middle-aged lama has probably repeated the spell of his special protector-god millions of times. The average number for other Tibetans is five or ten turns of the beads daily. A unique feature of Tibetan prayer beads is that they do more than merely register prayers. Hanging from the prayer beads, besides the two insignias of the monk—the *dorje* and the bell—are often odd objects like keys, tweezers, and a metal toothpick. In the story *Kim* by Rudyard Kipling, the lama whom Kim reveres uses his prayer beads as a measuring chain.

A Tibetan monk owns very little, usually just his clothes and prayer beads. Even though he strives to be unattached to material things, a monk may cherish his prayer beads. One Buddhist abbot of a large and wealthy monastery possessed rosaries of pearls, emeralds, rubies, sapphires, coral, amber, crystal, and lapis lazuli.

The act of telling the beads is called *tang-che*, which means to purr like a cat. The soft repetition of prayers sounds like purring. The one prayer popular above all others is the prayer *Om! Man-ni pad-ma Hum!* It means "Hail! The Jewel in the Lotus!" an invocation similar to the Catholic "Hail Mary." The jewel in the lotus refers to Chenrezi, Tibet's patron-god, who was born in a lotus blossom. Since Tibetans say it so often, it may be the most frequently recited prayer in all the world.

Prayer beads never gained great popularity in China but are widespread in Japan. A Japanese teahouse always has a hook on which customers hang their prayer beads while they eat. These rosaries consist of 112 beads divided into two parts by two larger "parent" beads. One of these is called the Buddha bead. From it extends two strings. Each has twenty-one small beads and a long dewdrop bead. Hanging from the other parent bead, called the mother bead, are three strings. Two have five small beads and end with a dewdrop, and the third has ten beads and no dewdrop.

The 112 beads on the main string refer to different gods and saints. Except for the group of ten used simply as counters, the smaller beads on the short strings stand for followers of the Buddha. The dewdrops represent the four rulers who govern the four quarters of the universe. *Namu Amida Butsu*, "Hail Eternal Buddha," is the prayer sentence. This phrase is uttered so often that it has a shortened form—*Nembutsu*.

Simple Japanese prayer beads are made from cherry or plum wood. Fancy ones come in crystal, ivory, mother-of-pearl, jade, and even silver or gold. One of rattley dried seedpods is called women's tongues. The shapes of the beads are varied too. Besides round globes there are cylinders, skull-shaped beads, and figures of saints, the lotus, fish, birds, and pagodas.

During a prayer of request to a god, the rosary is held with one cross turn in it, like a figure eight. Its loops rest on the middle fingers of both hands. The hands are then brought together until the fingertips touch. With the beads lying in between, the hands are raised slowly to the forehead. During the prayer the beads on the loops and the others on the string are rubbed up and down, making a grating noise. Some devotees do this very energetically.

The Nichiren, an unusually militant group of Japanese Buddhists, have a prayer ceremony called *Go Ki-to* in which the prayer beads are handled differently. Because they are slightly flattened, the Nichiren beads are called oranges. In the ceremony the string is tied to a small wooden sword about five inches long. The large beads are fastened near the point. On the sword are written a creed and prayers. A monk holds the sword in his right hand. He makes nine passes in the air with the sword. On each swing he repeats part of the creed. These nine strokes portray a Japanese character, *miyo*, meaning mysterious, wonderful, that is drawn with nine brushstrokes. The

● Strands of Buddhist rosaries.

other monks chant the prayer to fit the short, jerky meter of the sword cutting the air. The beads clacking against the sword at every swing marks the proper time.

About six hundred years after the birth of Jesus, the prophet Muhammad roused the people of Arabia to a strong faith in one God, Allah, and to obedience to his laws. Muhammad's followers called the new faith Islam, meaning submission. They called themselves Muslims, meaning those who submit to the will of Allah. Muslims pray five times a day and love to repeat the ninety-nine "beautiful names" of Allah.

From the Hindus or Buddhists of India or the Christian monks of Syria, Muslims borrowed the practice of prayer beads. The prayer beads fit well the Muslim idea of Allah's ninety-nine names. Muslims included a bead for every divine name, making the string ninety-nine beads long, with a marker after each thirty-three. There is also a shorter set of thirty-three beads and a longer one of one thousand. Telling the beads consists of reciting the ninety-nine beautiful names of Allah in a low voice or silently. The beautiful names of Allah include merciful, forgiving, and creator. Muslims call their string of prayer beads a *subhah*, meaning to glorify Allah.

The two ends of the string of beads are passed through two small beads and then through a cylinder bead. They end in a knot or tassel that is black, red, or green silk. Some Muslims call the cylinder bead the minaret because it looks like the tower on a mosque. Others call it the *imam*, or prayer leader. This one-hundreth bead has a nickname too, the camel. The story is that the camel alone knows the one-hundredth name of God, yet it refuses to divulge it. This is why the camel looks so haughty and superior.

Materials most used are seeds, shells, jet, olive wood, olive pits, balsam, date pits, ivory, mother-of-pearl, horn, camel bone, chalcedony, and amber. Sometimes amber pieces are found having little insects or spiders trapped inside. Such a stone is polished to show off the rarity of the bead. *Subhahs* manufactured in the holy places of Mecca and Medina in Saudi Arabia, and Kerbela and Najaf in

Iraq are highly prized. When made of earth from Kerbela, prayer beads are believed by Muslims of the Shiite sect to turn red on the anniversary of their martyr's death.

The string of one thousand beads is used only for one occasion, the ceremony of the *Subhah*. This ceremony is part of an eminent person's funeral. Some Muslims believe that the soul lingers for one night after burial before departing to Allah's throne to be judged. Mullahs, or priests, sometimes as many as fifty, gather at the deceased's home for three or four hours. One of them brings the thousand-bead *subhah*, enormous and heavy because each bead is the size of a pigeon egg. After reciting from memory certain chapters of the Koran, the Muslim's sacred book, the priests repeat three thousand times, "There is no God but Allah." One mullah holds the prayer beads and counts each repetition.

The *subhah* is also used in a special prayer for securing divine guidance. When a Muslim is uncertain about a choice in life, like whether to make a trip or what to do about an illness or what subject to study in school, he or she grasps the prayer beads and rubs them inside the palms of the hands. Next, the first chapter of the Koran is repeated. Then the user breathes upon the rosary in order to put the power of the sacred text into the beads. Finally the Muslim seizes one bead at random and counts towards the minaret at the tassel. "Allah, Muhammad, Abu Jahl [an enemy of the Prophet], Allah, Muhammad, Abu Jahl," he or she recites bead by bead until reaching the minaret. When the count ends with Allah, it means that the request will be granted, or a yes. If it ends with Abu Jahl, the answer is no, the request is denied. If Muhammad is the last bead before the minaret, the reply is maybe.

Not all strings of beads in the Middle East are put to religious use. Especially among people living along the Mediterranean Sea, *subhahs* are worry beads or conversation beads or idle beads for nervous fingers. Even while walking, Turks and Greeks finger the beads in their pockets. After work and on days-off, men in the countries along the Mediterranean coast crowd into coffee houses to gossip and argue. The *tump tump tump* of worry beads keeps rhythm with the conversation. The type of worry beads advertises the type of man who clasps them in his lap. A wealthy merchant may have worry beads of olive pits, an emblem of his economical ways. A flashy newcomer to a Kabul (Afghanistan) cafe may sport beads of turquoise. In Turkish towns, farmers carry worry beads made of mashed rose petals that have been rolled like clay and sun-dried. From the fingers of members of old Iranian families hang beads from Persepolis, the ancient capital of Iran. Most prized of the Persepolis beads are chalcedony, swirled and spotted with white. Like the West Africans and their aggries, Iranians hope their Persepolis beads adorned a king of long ago.

ABACUS
(PLURAL: ABACI)

8 Nippon Steel of Japan produces twenty-eight million tons of steel products per year. It is easily the world's largest steel manufacturer. In its New York office high above Park Avenue, the treasurer, Mr. Kawakatsu, keeps track of Nippon Steel sales to America. In charge of recording millions of dollars of business, the Japanese businessman does most of the accounting on his soroban, a Japanese abacus.

His soroban is very simple. It is thirteen inches long, four inches high, and has twenty-six rows of five beads each. The rows of beads are separated into "heaven" and "earth" by a divider that runs lengthwise one inch from the top. In "heaven" resides one bead worth five times as much as each of the four on "earth." For example, in the units row each of the beads on "earth" is worth one and the bead in "heaven" is worth five. In the tens column, the beads in the lower section are worth ten each and the single bead in the upper part is worth fifty.

When a bead is pushed toward the partition between "earth" and "heaven," it is in a counting position. A soroban showing the number 573 would look like this: In the units row, three "earth" beads are pushed up; in the tens row, the heaven bead worth fifty is pushed down and two earth beads worth ten each are pushed up; in the hundreds row, the top bead is pushed down.

Sitting in his modern office decorated with large potted plants and abstract paintings, Mr. Kawakatzu is surprised when we ask why he uses the simple bead calculator instead of an electronic one. "Obviously the soroban is easier to use, and faster," he replies. "In our main offices in Tokyo, hundreds of bookkeepers and accountants rely on their sorobans for speed and accuracy. Japan makes more electronic calculators than any other country, but Japanese people who work with numbers rely on the soroban. For adding and subtracting and most multiplication and division, electronics cannot match it."

Until two hundred years ago, Europeans and Americans did their arithmetic with counters on boards, not with pen and paper. In fact, the word "abacus" comes from the Greek *abax*, meaning table

● Accountants at the main office of Nippon Steel Corporation in Tokyo. For most arithmetic operations, the soroban is faster and more accurate than the electronic calculator, provided one is skilled at using it.

or flat surface. Here is how a counter board works. On a flat surface, draw parallel lines, one for each unit of measure. Three lines would represent ones, tens, and hundreds. The number 263 would be shown as

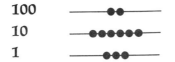

The Greeks and Romans often used pebbles as counters. The Latin word for pebble is *calculus*, which gives us our word "calculate." Doing a calculation meant putting the pebbles in the right places.

The secret of counter-board arithmetic is grouping numbers. When you have ten ones, you replace them with one ten. When you have ten hundreds, you replace them with a one-thousand counter. Suppose you want to add 9 + 19. First you put nine counters on the ones line. When you add the first of the nine 1's of 19, you have 10 on the units line. These counters you remove and replace with one counter on the tens line. The eight remaining 1's now fit on the ones line. The remaining 10 of 19 is added by placing another counter on the tens line. The final result is

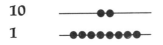

showing 28.

The Romans would have done this problem the same way but with Roman numbers. They also made the abacus easier to read by sticking a place in between the lines where a fives measure could be placed. If you show 28 as

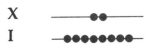

it is hard at a glance to count so many counters on the ones line. To make it easier to read, the Romans showed 28 as

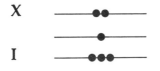

The counter in between the I and X lines equals V. The amount shown on the board would be written XXVIII, just as it is shown. This practice continued among Europeans during the Middle Ages and the Renaissance. The number 263 that we earlier represented as

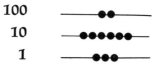

is more easily read if we place the counters

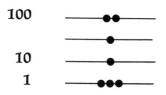

Until Europeans adopted Arabic numbers from the Arabs, all calculations were done on an abacus. Even today the British treasury is called the Exchequer because treasury officials used to count money on a large table that had checks, or squares, for different types of money. On one square, the treasurer kept track of pennies, on another shillings, on another pounds, on another tens of pounds, and so forth. When the shillings square had twenty counters on it, the accountant would remove them and add one counter to the pounds square, for twenty shillings equal a pound. In this way sums of money could be added and subtracted without crowding the board with counters and without losing track of what had been added previously.

This counting-board abacus worked well for figuring out taxes. Let's say that back in 1600, Mr. Wink owned ten horses, five hundred cows, and nine hundred sheep. Let's set the tax rate at three shillings per horse, three pence per cow, and one penny per sheep. Once a year an Exchequer official visited Mr. Wink's farm. Together they would count the animals. For each horse, the Exchequer man placed three counters in the shillings square. When he had counted all the horses, there would be thirty counters in the shillings square.

Since twenty shillings equal one pound, the tax collector would remove twenty counters from the shillings space and replace them with just one counter in the pounds square. This made one pound, ten shillings.

On the five hundred cows, Mr. Wink owed the government fifteen hundred pence. Since twelve pence equal one shilling, every time the tax man accumulated twelve counters in the penny square, he removed them and placed one counter in the shillings square. Eventually there would be 125 counters in the shillings square, except that every twenty counters in that space could be replaced by one counter in the pounds square. So the cow tax came to six pounds, five shillings, and no pence. Horses plus cows then added up to seven pounds, fifteen shillings. How would the tax on sheep end up on the Exchequer's table? (The answer is written upside down at the bottom of the page.) As you can see, the abacus can group in numbers of twelve and twenty as easily as ten.

When the tax on horses, cows, and sheep had been calculated, the tax collector counted the number of counters in the various squares and wrote the total on a piece of paper. In 1600, Arabic numbers were still strange to most people. So the tax collector would write for Mr. Wink the total tax due in both Roman numbers and Arabic: XI £.10s. or 11£.10s. The way the sum was written was completely independent of the way in which it was calculated. In order to do tax arithmetic, you needed to know only how many pennies were in a shilling, how many shillings in a pound. The abacus did the calculating.

Of course, in 1600, just as now, people did a lot of arthmetic in their heads. But when the problem was too long or too complicated, Mr. Wink, the officials of the Exchequer, and others who depended on numbers did their arithmetic on a counting board. It was not until the late 1700s and early 1800s that Arabic numbers became

Abacus
(Plural: Abaci)

Three pounds, fifteen shillings, and no pence.

popular, and shopkeepers, householders, and governments learned how to add, subtract, multiply, and divide by the pen-reckoning we now learn in school.

Today most people in Asia still do their calculations on the abacus. If you have a Chinese restaurant in your neighborhood, ask the owner whether he keeps his accounts with an abacus called a *suan pan*, meaning calculator tray. Like the Japanese soroban, this abacus has beads that slide on a rod. But instead of one bead in "heaven" and four beads on "earth," the *suan pan* has two beads on top and five below.

The Chinese probably took the idea of a bead abacus from the Romans. Like the Greeks before them and the Europeans after, the Romans did most of their calculations with pebble (in Latin, *calculus*) counters. But they also invented a hand-size frame abacus that held small beads in narrow slots. A Roman merchant could carry this abacus on a journey. The nine rows of beads, divided like the soroban into one upper and four lower, enabled him to calculate large enough figures to do business.

Fixing the beads in a movable file seemed like an excellent idea to the Chinese, who made it more sophisticated in two ways. First, they put the beads on a rod. Second, and most important, they used a number system based on ten, so that the rods represented (from right to left) units, tens, hundreds, and so forth.

The Chinese used the *suan pan* so much they thought of it as a servant. And some Chinese saw their servants as abaci. A text from the time of Kublai Khan (the 1200s) compares servants to types of beads. A new servant who works when ordered and without a beating is like a mortar bead that crushes herbs and other kinds of medicine. This large bead does its work thoroughly and remains unharmed by the pharmacist. The second type of servant works when **Beadazzled** ordered but must be beaten. This type is like an abacus bead that the **68** owner must flick up and down on the rod in order to do its work. The third type of servant was a sour-faced bead. This person remains idle if ordered and even if beaten. Women wore sour-faced beads as charms against evil spirits.

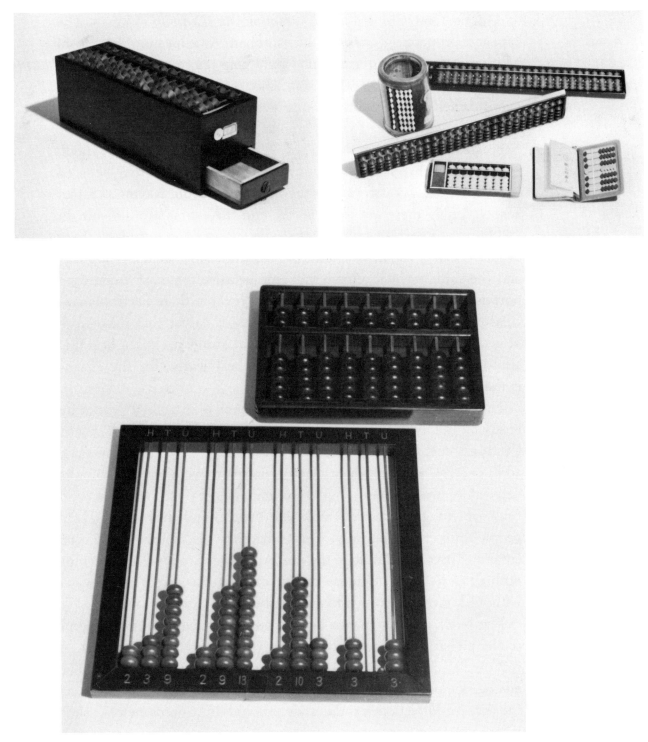

● A variety of sorobans commonly used in Japan today.

Around 1600, Chinese merchants took the *suan pan* to Japan. The Japanese pronounced *suan pan* like soroban. An educator, Shigeyoshi Mori, saw how much the abacus would help his country. He opened an abacus school. Students of this school introduced the soroban to every corner of the country and to every class of citizens. By 1700, everybody who worked with numbers owned a soroban. When our Nippon Steel executive, Mr. Kawakatsu, went to soroban school, there were eight grades of achievement, like the different belts of karate. Mr. Kawakatsu rose to the fifth level before leaving soroban school. Today there are three levels, and the exams are difficult. In 1978, over three million students studied soroban in business school or in special soroban academies. Soroban classes remain popular, and the skills learned remain valuable because for most accounting purposes, sorobans are faster and more reliable than electronic calculators. Even if a student does not follow a career that makes use of a soroban, the mental skills learned in soroban classes help the student to think logically and to remember clearly, for the abacus is the thinking person's computer.

The type of computer we see most often is digital. It works by receiving numbers and putting them into a program or pathway of electronic circuits that performs a certain kind of calculation—say, addition. The way in which electric pulses move along the circuits determines the answer. Digital computers are fast, versatile, and compact. But they do not think like people, and they do not help people think more logically. This is because the method the digital computer uses is invisible to the eye. All we see are input and results, nothing in between. Using a pocket calculator is like driving a car without knowing about internal combustion.

The other kind is an analog computer. Its method is analogous to the physical laws that govern the visible universe around us. A

rod or dial or some other variable object measures the input. The analog computer performs different arithmetic tasks by changing the size or direction of the rods or wheels. Speedometers, slide rules, and abaci are analog computers.

The beads of a soroban must be moved, like the second type of Kublai Khan's servants. The beads form a pattern that changes as we supply more input. The soroban remembers what we did and adjusts to new information. The answer takes shape before our eyes. In the hands of a soroban master, the answer comes so quickly that it is difficult to see. But you can slow the abacus down. The answer appears logically, in a natural pattern, not mysteriously in lights on a screen.

We watched Mr. Kawakatsu gracefully flick the beads up and down as he works on million-dollar accounts. When praised for his style, he says that he is just an average sorobaner. "I'm not being modest. At the Tokyo accounting office, there are sorobaners, usually women, so good at this that they don't have to use the soroban. For many problems, they see the beads move in their mind's eye. This mental moving of the beads happens so quickly that they just write down what they see in their brains. In a sense, part of their brains have become sorobans. They never make mistakes." That is the beauty of the soroban, an analog computer that thinks with beads.

EMBROIDERY FROM HEAD TO TOE

9 Many clothes of the Near East have had beads on them. In ancient times, Pharaoh Tutankhamen wore a skullcap embroidered with beads. Upper-class Egyptians wrapped the bodies of their dead in nets of tube beads we know as "mummy beads." Ishtar, the Babylonian goddess of love and war, was said to have had a bead necklace of lapis lazuli and gold. In the Babylonian flood story, when the waters recede Ishtar swears by her bead necklace that the world will never again be ruined by flood. In the era of Islam, royalty and courtiers of Persia and Turkey liked to wear flowing robes, stiff fitted jackets, and turned-up shoes, all embroidered with beads. The robe of a shah or a pasha might be covered with beads of precious stones and pearls. The slippers of a wealthy merchant would have embroidery of glass beads on silver and gold thread.

In Europe, beads were put on necklaces long before they were sewed to clothes. New excavations of an early Iron Age settlement in Yugoslavia have turned up glass-bead necklaces of many colors, sizes, and patterns. Most of these objects are found in the graves of women. It was only in medieval times that Europeans began to put beads on clothes, but only on ceremonial costumes of the church and state. The coronation mantle of the Holy Roman Emperor, dating from 1134, is enriched with seed pearls. Priests in thirteenth-century

73

England and Germany wore vestments whose bead embroidery told stories taken from the lives of saints and the Bible. Some prayer books had lavish bindings adorned with pictures done in tiny beads of glass, coral, and gold. These religious pictures took their designs from oil paintings. For the faces of figures, seed pearls were used.

There were several periods in Europe and America when beads were fashionable. The first, from 1630 to 1680, came when the production of glass beads in Venice, Bohemia, and the Netherlands peaked. Most of these beads traveled to Africa and America to be traded for slaves, rum, and beaver pelts. Other beads stayed home and were used to make objects as well as to decorate clothes. Europeans constructed whole vases, hair ornaments, and candlesticks from beads strung on wire. Most popular of all was the beaded basket, also known as the baby basket because it sometimes held baby's linen. The baskets were rectangular, shallow, and the size of candy boxes. The beads were strung on wire and fashioned into a kind of stiff bead lace that was bound to an iron or brass frame.

Also fashionable were bead bouquets. Tulips, honeysuckle, roses, or fruits, berries, and nuts were composed with beads on wire and then woven into baskets with strands of silk. Some of the beads were so small that no needle could pass through the eye. To thread these tiny seed beads, a needlewoman dipped the tip of the thread into shellac to make a stiff point. At the bottom of the basket, she embroidered in beads a picture of more flowers, a landscape, or a portrait of the reigning monarch.

Other objects combined embroidery with beadwork. Needleworkers of the seventeenth century took up the cabinetmaker's trade of decorating boxes, cabinets, and mirror frames. Where the woodworker might carve or inlay or paint, the beadworker wove bead designs on green satin and tacked them to the wood. Today glass is cheap and frames expensive, but in the seventeenth century frames were easy to come by and glass was scarce and costly. When a mirror broke, the owner would try to salvage a piece and put it in a new, wide frame. Around the small piece of mirror glass, crafts-

● A Victorian pin cushion from Devon, England. Beads and sequins frame the initials "ME" on the top and insignias in the center.

men made the frame as eye-catching as possible, often with bugle and large seed beads.

Bead embroidery also set the fashion in purses during the 1600s. Gentlewomen passed the time by making purses of colored beads sewn on mesh. Bearing mottoes such as "The Gift of a Friend" or "Be Not Too Free," the purses were big enough to hold gloves, or keys, or a hand mirror, but only one thing at a time.

Skirts in the eighteenth century were tucked and full and had side pockets. So it is understandable why bead purses were so small. But even after 1800, when dress styles fit close to the body and abandoned pockets altogether, women's bags remained small and impractical. One kind of purse made of mesh fabric was called a reticule, from the French word meaning net. Practical-minded people, noting how little the bag carried, called it a ridiculous. Many reticules were netted with colored seed beads.

Skirts became wide and swishing again in the 1830s and women continued to use bags. In the 1840s, women carried dark-blue or black velvet drawstring bags embroidered with steel beads and trimmed with beaded tassels. Steel, then a new material, was as admired in jewelry and decoration as it is in skyscrapers today. After the middle of the century steel and gilt beads and sequins replaced colored beads on Victorian stocking purses, silk tubes eight to ten inches long. The beads were either threaded onto the silk of the purse or woven in crossstitch on the surface. Women wore their fringed bead bags hanging from a loop at the waistband.

In 1861, after the death of Prince Albert, England was plunged into mourning. Queen Victoria herself did not alter her heavy, somber mourning clothes for over twenty years. Following the queen's example, women favored clothes of black crepe and jewelry of jet, a black semiprecious gemstone. In 1873, two hundred workshops in London were cutting jet into round, bugle, or faceted beads. Women wore sprays of jet beads in their hair. The Victorian lady liked to wear a neckband adorned with a single bit of jet or an engraved jet cameo mounted on a ribbon. Or she might wear three rows of jet beads on her neck with a low-cut gown, her shoulders masked in black gauze.

Jet beads came in three types. First, there was fossilized driftwood, or true jet. Victorians named this Whitby after rosaries used by monks at Whitby Abbey in Yorkshire, England, where the best and hardest jet was mined. Second, there was French jet, an imitation made of polished glass. The third kind, called ebonite, or composition, was light-weight and less brilliant. Made by pressing together rubber and sulfur in a mold, it was an early form of plastic available to people who could not afford Whitby or French.

In America, the end of the Civil War brought extravagance in clothing. Women wore much bead trim on both daytime and evening clothes. Beaded braid and fringe trimmed necklines and hems, collars and cuffs, sleeves and shoulder epaulettes. American women drew their models for gowns from *Godey's Ladies Book*. This magazine was both a sewing pattern book and a mail-order catalogue. Finely etched hand-colored prints (the origin of the phrase "fashion plate") illustrated *Godey's*. These were so handsome they were often framed and hung.

Godey's of 1866 showed hats, tiaras, and hair combs with loops of coral, crystal, pearl, and especially jet beads. The beads wreathed the face like chains on a Christmas tree. *Godey's* advised: "The chains can fall under the chin or over the back of the neck at pleasure." Jet beads, black fringe, and passementerie, or bead-encrusted braid and cord, served to edge every article of clothing, wrapping ladies up like holiday packages.

Like women of the seventeenth century, nineteenth-century ladies beaded objects as well as clothes. Mirror frames, perfume bottles, and candlesticks were all encrusted with beads. Beaded window hangings hung in the bathhouses of some German castles, letting light pass through while giving bathers privacy. "German embroidery," which combined glass beads and embroidery in bright-colored wools, was especially popular all over Europe after 1850. Pattern-makers stamped on canvas pictures from famous bird books like John James Audubon's *Birds of America* (1827–38), and needlewomen put their parrots, macaws, and other richly plumed birds in wool on firescreens, cushions, and piano stools. Flowers were worked in white, crystal, gray, or black beads only, and set off against a striking royal-blue or scarlet background.

While gentlewomen beaded as a pastime and other women beaded to vary their wardrobes, thousands of women worked in the beading trade for wages. Like other garment workers, many beadworkers toiled in sweatshops under frightful conditions. They worked twelve hours a day, six days a week, in poorly lit, unhealthy shops for pennies an hour. For meager pay but under better conditions, other women did piecework in their homes. Shoemakers, milliners, and dressmakers sent them their work for trimming. By working fast, a woman could bead a shoe in a half-hour, or twenty-four pairs a day, and earn a dollar or so a week. This could buy the family the food twenty dollars might buy today. All kinds of beading was done by piecework—on jackets and capes, trimmings and braids, belts, shoes, and shoe buckles. It was a terrible hardship when beads went out of fashion for a season, a year, or longer. And the careers of many women were cut short because sorting the sizes, colors, and shapes,

● One of a pair of satin shoes, designed by Roger Vivier for Christian Dior in 1960, covered with transparent peacock-blue beads and clear rhinestones.

and threading and sewing the beads in dimly lit rooms damaged their eyes.

In the 1890s, day dresses became more practical, but evening clothes were magnificent. A dressy evening costume of 1890 was black chiffon and silk. It had a net train flowing from high on the back, embroidered with beads in swirling designs. The beads were silvered glass, jet, or crystal in varied shapes and sizes—bugles, domes, flat, buttons. High-heeled shoes of the era were made of soft kid leather and were often decorated with bronze, gilt, silvery, and jet beads and fastened with an ankle button.

In the 1890s there were foreign influences in bead necklaces. The "Cleopatra" was a row of turquoise from which hung a fringe of coral, agate, and other beads. A "Gypsy" necklace was a double row of turquoise and coral beads mingled with gold pieces and had three amulets as pendants, which were fringed with more beads. An "African" necklace was strung with amber beads, set off with red silk tassels.

The craze for costume jewelry began after World War I. All sorts and lengths of bead necklaces came into fashion. Short pearl necklaces with pearl button earrings were especially popular. Coco Chanel, a Parisian fashion designer, introduced colored glass jewelry, still popular today. She also created the fashion of wearing many ropes of artificial pearls for contrast with a simple tailored suit or dress.

In the 1920s came a new, briefer age of the bead. An exciting new dance style, the Charleston, was invented in 1924. With the coming of fast dancing, hemlines rose. When quick-stepping couples did their stuff on the dance floor, the panels on the women's shifts flapped—"flappers," the dancers were nicknamed, after a sporting term for young partridges, who likewise move their wings fast and furiously. The twenties evening frocks were heavily beaded and sequined. Trailing patterns in gilt, coral, black, and silver were used most often, for they sparkled under dance-hall lights.

Not only bodices and skirts but hemlines boasted beads, often scalloped, in petals, or arrows. The beads and sequins were often combined with machine embroidery on fine crepe and georgette. Machine-stitched and beaded garments were bought ready to sew up. Each bead had to be sewn on separately. Otherwise a broken thread could rain beads all over the dance floor.

In the 1950s in America, beads with only one hole were as big a fad as Hula-Hoops. Using "pop-it" beads, a girl could make as long a necklace as she wished by popping bead after bead together—beginning to end. When new, the pop-its were lovely pearly pink, yellow, green, blue, and white colors.

In the 1960s and 1970s many young people became interested in different life styles. Some of the new generation traveled to Eastern countries such as India, Nepal, and Afghanistan to try out a slower pace of life. As a result, the so-called hippies took to wearing bead-embroidered tunics from Asia over long skirts or blue jeans. Other student-age Americans followed suit.

The word "jeans" is derived from the name of the Italian city Genoa. In the Middle Ages, the textile industry of Genoa produced a heavy blue twill cotton fabric that Italian sailors wore as pants. When the Italians docked in French ports, other workers admired their soft, durable pants and sought their own jeans—*de Genes* (meaning from Genoa). The French began producing the same fabric in Nîmes. When asked, the French sailors said it was *de Nîmes*, meaning from Nîmes. English-speakers heard this as denim. So we now say we are wearing jeans made of denim.

In the 1970s everybody put on a pair of jeans. They also wore jackets, bags, and boots made of denim cloth. Clothes made of denim broke into high fashion. Instead of throwing away worn and torn jeans, it became a fad to patch them. Women recycled old jeans by cutting the seams and resewing the pants as a long skirt.

Glass beads joined the jeans scene. On the East Side of Manhattan, decorated jeans became the rage. Beads, fabric appliqué, steel studs, sequins, lace, and acrylic painting adorned every part of a pair of jeans. Geraldo Rivera, a television personality, used to arrive at fashionable night spots wearing flashy jeans. His favorite pair had one leg in plain denim; the other leg, from waist to cuff, like a totem pole, had bands of appliqué, seed, shell, and pearl beads, bead pendants, and embroidery, with large aggries down the outside seam.

East Siders vied for the wildest jeans reputation. Andy Warhol showed up at black tie dinners in faded jeans and a denim jacket that had big cloud patches made out of cloth. Gloria Vanderbilt started out carrying a denim handbag with leather patches outlined in beads. One thing led to another. Ms. Vanderbilt went into business, and her name is now on the seat of women's high-fashion jeans.

In New York City during the eighties, to buy beautifully ornamented denim clothing a person might go to Serendipity, of all things an ice-cream parlor. On the ground floor of Serendipity, shoppers relax over big bowls of ice cream, exotic sundaes, elegant parfaits, and hot chocolate billowing with whipped cream. Upstairs denim-lovers pull on jeans, jackets, vests, caftans, skirts made from recycled jeans, and broad-brimmed hats, all denim. Those able to afford them order custom-made clothes. Geraldo Rivera's pants cost several hundred dollars in 1973.

The boutique has made unique designs for Cher, Tab Hunter, Willis Reed, and many other sports, television, and film stars. Stephen Bruce, the designer of many of these clothes, is known as the Dali of Denim. One of his gorgeous creations is a long A-line denim skirt entitled "Las Vegas." On its front and back panels sway floor-show dancers. Price made their bikinis out of sequins and outlined their figures in pearl beads. Richard Burton's then girl friend bought it. To do-it-yourselfers the boutique offers jeans decorating kits of studs, needlework, and beads.

In 1980, a fashion started of weaving glass beads right into the hair. The fashion was inspired by the movie *10*, in which Bo Derek wore her hair worked all over in tiny braids. It can take over three hours to do the braiding, and some *coiffeurs* have gone into the style as their exclusive business. A pot of beads sits next to the bobby pins, rollers, and elastics. Once woven, this hairstyle is as long-lasting as any permanent. Before Bo Derek made it popular, this was an Afro-American hairdo. Many young black Americans have reclaimed this use of beads. Their brightly beaded braids continue a heritage of beads and dazzling adornment that goes back to their African origins.

● In 1980, this Afro-American beaded hairstyle found new popularity. A style full of beads takes hours to braid.

Pharaoh Tutankhamen's vulture collar. The ancient Egyptians considered glass a precious substance. The vulture's wings are composed of 250 metal plaques inlaid with hundreds of pieces of colored glass. *(Courtesy of Lee Bolton)*

A carved cinnabar bead. Cinnabar is a mineral ore that fuses when heated but remains soft enough to carve. *(Photo by Wendy Chesebrough)*

Eye beads. This type of design is found all over the world. It usually includes a spot circumscribed by rings, but may be more stylized like the eye beads here. *(Photo by Jonathan Lanman)*

Syrian trade-wind beads. *(Photo by Jonathan Lanman)*

Millefiori bead. *(Photo by Jonathan Lanman)*

The chevron or aggry bead is made by building up a cylinder of several layers of colored glass. The bead-maker then grinds the barrel to expose inner layers, making a star or chevron design. *(Photo by Jonathan Lanman)*

Amber beads. Amber is the petrified resin from a now extinct pine tree that grew along the Baltic Sea. Because of their mysterious golden glow the beads were valued highly as traders brought them south to Greeks and other Mediterranean people as early as 1600 B.C. *(Photo by Jonathan Lanman)*

● Assorted trade-wind beads. The large disk-shaped bead *(right)* is a wire-wound Zanzibar bead. The bumpy bead *(far left)* is a crumb bead, made by rolling a glass bead, still hot and soft, over "crumbs" of glass. *(Photo by Jonathan Lanman)*

● Blue and white Dutch trade-wind beads. Traders carried these on ropes three or four feet long and weighing several pounds. *(Photo by Wendy Chesebrough)*

Peddler dolls were popular in England and America in the 1800s. Their baskets overflowed with miniature notions, candy medicines, sequins, yarns, and beads. *(Courtesy of the Bethnel Green Museum)*

A Dutch bead garden in Broek, a small village just north of Amsterdam. *(Courtesy of The Netherlands Open Air Museum)*

● A Zulu girl from the Transkei, South Africa, adorned with beads. *(Courtesy of Alice Mertens)*

A late nineteenth-century green silk parasol. The beaded handle and knob display human figures and leaf designs. *(Photo by Joshua Green)*

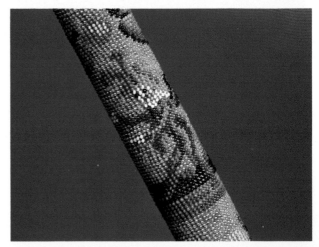

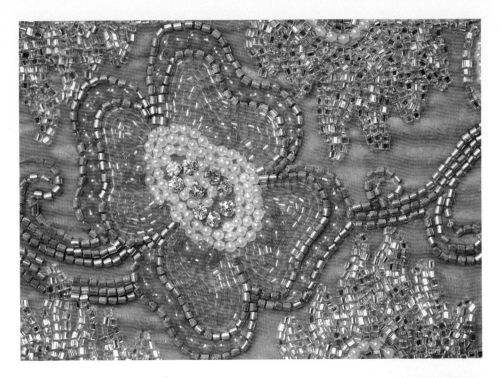

This flapper dress was designed by Paul Poiret of Paris in the 1920s. Rhinestones and pearls, as well as gold and rose bugle beads are sewn over gold lamé. *(Photo by Joshua Green)*

A bead rose in progress, showing wire spool, individual leaf and petal, and finished rose. *(Photo by David Bliwas)*

CRAFT
PROJECTS

INTRODUCTION

As you have seen, beads are meant to be handled. Wampum beads passed from hand to hand as money. People of all religions slip prayer beads through their hands as they pray. The most prized aggry beads are those that have been polished smooth by generations of hands. Zulu love necklaces are woven by hand, and even in the modern world of computers, many people still perform calculations, by hand, on an abacus or soroban.

The craft projects section of *Beadazzled* puts your own hands to work. In this section, you have an opportunity to make many of the various types of beads and bead-related objects described in the book thus far. The crafts are arranged in order from the easiest to the most difficult. You can make the trade-bead necklace in less than an hour. Rose petal beads take a little longer. The bow drill and abacus require a friend to work with you, and the beaded notebook cover and bead rose demand more patience and time. In any case, the finished projects, which require the simplest of tools and materials, will provide you with a greater understanding of beads and bead work and, in many cases, a beautiful gift for a friend.

TRADE-BEAD
NECKLACE

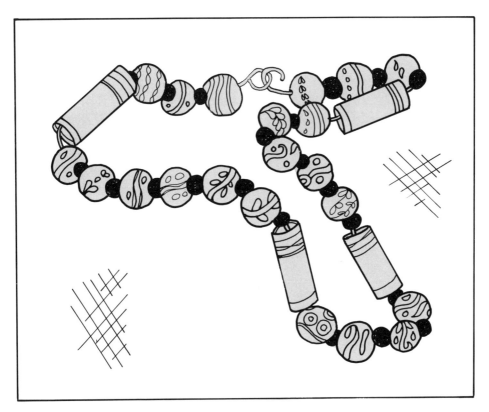

EQUIPMENT YOU WILL NEED:

Matchsticks
Small paintbrush
Sharp-nosed pliers (optional)

MATERIALS YOU WILL NEED:

#16 soft brass wire, at least 18 in.
Package of oven-bake clay
A few wooden store-bought beads
Tempera paints
Clear shellac

DIRECTIONS:

1. Shape clay beads and punch a hole through each one with a matchstick or something similiar.

2. Bake the clay beads as directed on package and paint. (You can also stain the wooden beads in strong coffee or tea).

3. Let the decorated beads dry, then shellac them. (This will prevent the colors from running on your clothes.)

4. Shape the wire into a circle to fit like a collar around your neck.

5. String on the beads.

6. With your fingers (or sharp-nosed pliers if you have them), bend the ends of the wire at the back of the necklace so they make two hooks for fastening.

● A shop in New York City called Glori Bead has bins and bowls of beads from many lands. For a lucky bead of a design Africans still wear, write to them at 172 West 4th Street, New York, New York 10011. They have fish bone, monkey bone, clamshell, bauxite, ivory, cowrie, and coconut-shell beads from Africa. For one dollar they will send you about a half-dozen. Or for the same price you can have a big millefiori, an Egyptian scarab, or a lacquered cinnabar bead from China. You must enclose a self-addressed stamped envelope with your order.

Try mixing in beads from broken or discarded necklaces. Exchange beads with friends and pen pals. That way your necklace will have a history all its own!

ROSE-PETAL
BEADS

EQUIPMENT YOU WILL NEED:

Enamel pot or a double boiler
Thimble or a very small scoop

MATERIALS YOU WILL NEED:

Rose petals—enough to make one heaping cup when firmly packed
One cup salt
Florist's wire
Dental floss, button thread, or fine elastic cord
Rose oil or rose perfume, sold at import gift shops

DIRECTIONS:

1. Gather petals of garden roses, or ask the florist to save you a bag of petals.

2. Shred the petals with your fingers. Combine in pot with the salt; mash well with a spoon.

3. Add 1/2 c. water and heat over a low flame, stirring constantly, until you have a smooth, dense paste.

4. Mix in a teaspoon or two of the rose oil or perfume.

5. With a rolling pin, roll out the paste like a piecrust on a board to about 1/4-in. thickness.

6. Cut out little rounds with the thimble or scoop, and roll the bits of pulpy dough in the palm of your hand to make balls.

7. String beads on florist's wire. Hang the wire in a cool, dry spot until beads dry. (This takes a few days.) Move beads occasionally to keep the holes free.

8. String the beads. For a necklace, make sure the length of thread you use is long enough to pass over your head. Using the elastic cord, you can make a bracelet or anklet without any clasp.

● The beads will be a dullish color. You can brighten the strand with dyed beads of other natural substances. Try steeping dried pumpkin seeds in coffee or a strong herbal tea. Varnish them and pierce. String rose-petal and pump-kin-seed beads in an alternating arrangement, several pumpkin-seed beads to every rose-petal bead.

MINIATURE
BEAD GARDENS

MATERIALS YOU WILL NEED:

Small fish tank, goldfish bowl or a big, wide-necked glass jar
   turned on its side
Sterilized potting soil
Vermiculite
Peat moss
Charcoal granules (the hard type—not barbeque briquettes)
Pebbles
Piece of clear plastic or glass cut to partially (about three-quarters)
   cover the container
Large seed beads, size E, three or four colors (maybe tulip
   colors like yellow, red, and orange)
Plants that are miniatures or that thrive when 2–6 in. in size, such as:
   Moss (can be found in backyards, in any forest, and
      on the benches in greenhouses)
   Artillery plant
   Prayer plant
   Sensitive plant (looks like tiny palm tree)
   Dwarf palm
   Brake and sword ferns
   Strawberry geranium
   Caladium
   Selaginella and peperomia (grows on chunks of rock)
   Miniature ivy
   Pileas like aluminum plant
   Small begonias like Dewdrop or Peridot
   Fittonia and baby's tears (for carpeting)

● Often pet stores and department stores sell leaky fish tanks at a big discount. If the crack is big, seal it with clear cement. A bead garden can be made in any glass container that has, either when standing or when turned on its side, a wide area for planting.

DIRECTIONS:

1. Wash and dry the container. Begin by making a woodland terrarium. It can consist of a combination of tropical plants that you buy or start from houseplant clippings and temperate plants that you find outdoors around your home.

2. First, put one part sterilized potting soil, one part vermiculite, or builder's sand, and one part peat moss, finely sifted, in a big heavy plastic bag and mix by kneading with your hands. (Packaged soil mixes are also available.)

3. Pass the soil through a 1/2-in. screen, then place the mixture back in the plastic bag and add water until soil is moist but not soggy.

4. Cover the base of container with 3/4–2 in. of drainage material. This can be the sand or gravel, or broken glass, pebbles, or any other coarse material. It both helps the soil to drain and keeps it loose. Slope a hill from the rear or make a mound in one corner so the bead "floor" will be in view. Do this by shaping the drainage material and keeping the depth of the soil and subsoil even. (No more than about a quarter of the space in the container should be used for the subsoil and soil.)

5. Pour charcoal 1/2–1 in. deep in the container. Charcoal absorbs soil impurities and keeps a garden sweet-smelling. (Even though packaged soil mix may contain some charcoal, you should add more.)

6. Cover with a thin layer of peat moss or nest of Sphagnum moss.

7. Add about 1 1/2 in. soil mixture.

8. Make a plan before starting. The walls of the container are like the frame of a picture. Do not plant at

the borders of your garden where the leaves will push against the container. The plants will grow rapidly, so space them well. Arrange the plants to show off each one. Place low-lying plants like mosses at the front of the terrarium, tall plants like ferns at the back. Start with your largest plant. It usually works best to plant your highest point or your background first.

Or perhaps you have a tiny tree that has a deeper root system than most other terrarium plants. You should place it first on a high spot. Make a hole in your soil with a teaspoon where you want the tree seedlings placed. Gently tap the plant out of its pot and shake off some of the soil around the roots. Place it in the hole and carefully add soil around its roots, up to the original soil height on the stem. *Gently* tamp or press the soil around the stem so that the plant stands erect. Follow this procedure with all plants. Use a long poker like a dowel or stick to dig holes for later plantings, when you must work around other plants.

9. Keep the beaded plot small. An area 2 1/2 in. in circumference will take one hundred beads to cover, or the number generally sold in one and a half small packs. Sketch the bead design on a piece of paper first, or lay out the beads on a piece of felt before transferring them to the terrarium. You may want to prepare a bed of sand for the beads. Sprinkle a patch of sand through a funnel made of aluminum foil, place little rounded stones as a path leading to it, and then lay out the bead design.

10. Last, arrange moss in patches alongside the bead design and at the edges of the garden.

11. Sprinkle with water and firm the soil—do not pack—around plants a few times the first day. Stick your fingers in the soil. It should feel moist an inch down. The second or third day put on the cover, leaving a slight opening.

● The garden will probably not need watering for several months. Moisture doesn't escape as rapidly from a garden with a cover. Water it only if the soil feels dry or the plants look thirsty. Spray gently. A turkey baster, squirt bottle, or mister of the kind used to wash windows makes a good watering tool. If the soil becomes soggy and too much moisture collects, you will see droplets on the plants and running down the inside of the glass case. Remove the lid for a few days to allow the inside to dry out somewhat. Otherwise mildew and rot will occur. A slight fogging on the inside of glass means the moisture level is correct.

In general, terrariums need indirect light. Keep the terrarium in a spot with a good source of natural light, probably a northern exposure, and on the cool side. Rays of sun should not touch the terrarium container directly. Rotate the garden occasionally. If new leaves are pale yellow, there is too *little* light.

Flowering plants require much sunshine. If flowering plants (such as miniature African violets or a rex begonia) are included along with the leafy, extra light is needed. Either set the terrarium in more direct sunlight or put a grow light overhead. Mosses will not survive the additional light; other plants probably will.

Chlorinated tap water should be left in an open container overnight before it is used to let the chlorine gas escape. Rain or spring water is best because it has no chemical salts.

Most terrarium plants are not real miniatures. If left to their own devices, they will soon outgrow the container. Every month or so pinch or trim or snip the plants to keep them pretty and compact. To trim, you can use manicure scissors. Remove any decayed or faded flowers or leaves.

BOW DRILL

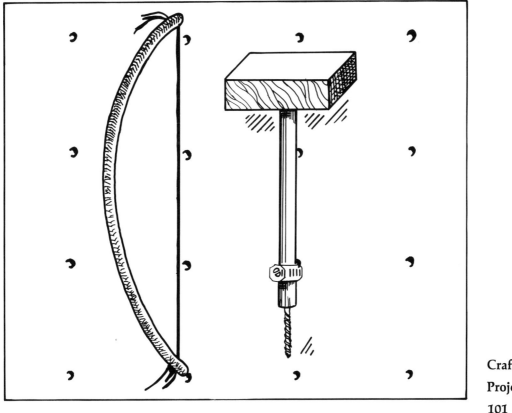

EQUIPMENT YOU WILL NEED:

Vise
Wood saw
Hand or electric drill
Drill bits, 1/16, 1/8, 3/16
Center punch
Hammer
Screwdriver

MATERIALS YOU WILL NEED:

Broomstick or dowel 7/8 in. in diameter
Hose clamp, size 10
Drill bit, 1/8
Square block of wood, approximately 3 1/2 in. on a side and
** 1 1/2 in. thick (these are the milled dimensions of a 2 in. x 4 in. board)**
one 10-penny nail 3 in. long
three 1/4-in. washers
one 3/8-in dowel 36 in. long
one rawhide shoelace at least 40 in. long

● This is a difficult project best done with someone handy with tools.

DIRECTIONS:

A. Making the shaft

1. Cut off a 10-in. length of broomstick or dowel.

2. Put the shaft upright in the vise; with the wood saw make two center cuts at right angles to each other, 2 in. deep if you are using broomstick, 2 1/2 in. deep for dowel.

3. Put the other end of the shaft upright in the vise; mark the center of the end with a punch; drill a 1/8-in. hole into the shaft. Take care to keep the drill perpendicular to the shaft so that the hole goes in straight.

4. Through the center of the square block of wood drill a 3/16-in. hole.

5. Put a 10-penny nail through the wood block; add three washers between the block and shaft; hammer the nail into the shaft until the nail head is almost flush with the top of the block of wood. (Because the hole in the wood is larger than the nail,

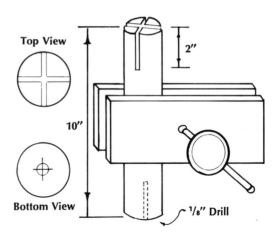

Top View

Bottom View

2"

10"

~ 1/8" Drill

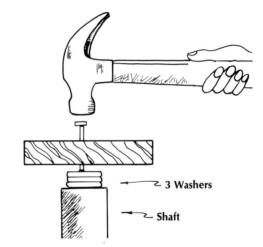

⤳ 3 Washers

⤳ Shaft

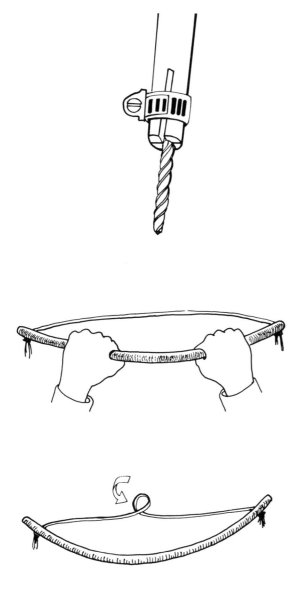

the shaft will turn freely while you hold the piece of wood in your hand. The washers reduce friction).

6. On the end of the shaft with the cross cuts, place a hose clamp and tighten just enough to keep it in place. The clamp and cross cuts act as a simple chuck. Put the 1/8-in. drill bit into the center of the cross cut; tighten the hose clamp to squeeze the end of the shaft tight on the drill bit.

B. Making the bow

1. Near each end of the 3/8-in. dowel carefully drill a 1/16-in. hole; enlarge it to 1/8 in. and then 3/16 in. with the other drill bits. (Drilling the 3/16-in. hole in three steps prevents splitting).

2. String the bow by slipping the ends of the rawhide through the holes in the dowel. Knot one end. Slightly flex the dowel and knot the other end of the rawhide to hold the dowel in a bowed position. (This takes *two* people: one holds the dowel in bent position and the other ties the knot.) Do not string the bow too tightly. You will need the extra flex to wrap the rawhide around the shaft.

C. Wrapping and drilling

1. Twist the rawhide around the shaft so that the point of crossover faces front. If this flexes the dowel too much, untie one end of the rawhide and make it a little longer. If the rawhide slips on the shaft, the bow should be tighter.

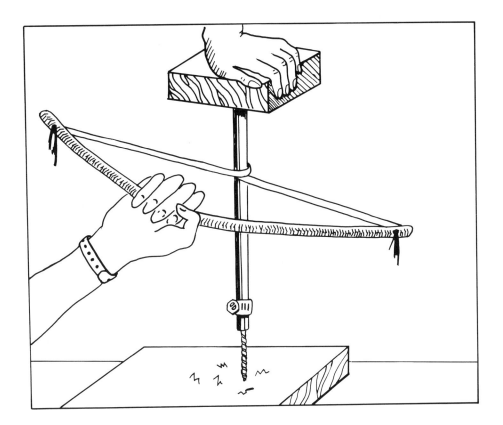

2. Stand a little to one side and move the bow back and forth with one hand while holding the wood block at the top of the shaft with the other hand.

● Try out your bowdrill on seeds such as chestnuts, acorns, Indian corn, or fruit pits such as peach and cherry pits, or pieces of soft or hard wood. (With an 1/8-in. bit you can easily drill through soft pine. For harder substances, start with a smaller bit.) Either hold the object to be drilled in a vise or have a friend hold it with pliers on a board. With the bowdrill you can pierce even a freshwater pearl. A professional craftsman today who uses the bowdrill for this last kind of drilling may set the pearls first in wax to hold them, because pearls are too delicate to put in a vise.

LOVE
NECKLACE

EQUIPMENT YOU WILL NEED:

One #9 needle
Scissors
Loom at least 17 in. long. If you buy a loom, follow directions
  for setting up. You can also make a loom from a picture frame
  or long boot box.

MATERIALS YOU WILL NEED:

One pack #3 white beads
Two or three packs #3 beads in other colors
One pack seed beads, white or soft pastel
One 1/2-in. bead
One spool heavy-duty white nylon thread
One spool white buttonhole thread
Graph paper
Cotton backing material, white, preferably Indian head fabric

DIRECTIONS:

A. Setting up the loom for making the necklace

1. Set three warp threads 1/8–3/16 in. apart. The loom should be at least 4 in. longer than necklace.

2. Double the first and last warp threads.

B. Weaving a two-bead-wide necklace

1. Plan the design on graph paper.

2. Use white and one other color #3 beads.

3. Cut a 24-in. length of nylon thread. Thread the needle.

4. With the loom horizontal in front of you, knot the nylon thread to the back warp thread at the left end of the loom. Leave at least 2 in. free warp between the end of the loom and the knotted thread. You will work from back to front and from left to right.

5. Take the first two beads according to your pattern. Position the

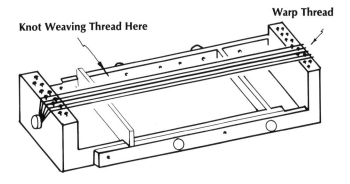

Knot Weaving Thread Here

Warp Thread

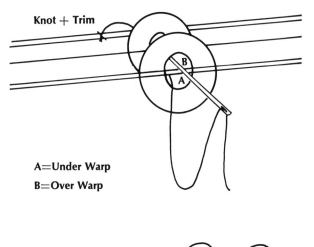

Knot + Trim

A=Under Warp
B=Over Warp

Knot + Trim

beads between the warp threads. Pass the needle back to front under warp threads and through beads. Return the needle over the warp threads and through the beads again. Repeat for each row.

6. When your beading thread becomes too short to weave easily, weave it back into the last three finished rows. Knot on the middle warp thread and trim carefully.

7. To add new thread, tie the end to the middle warp two rows back. Trim. Weave the thread through the finished rows to the start of a new row.

C. Finishing the necklace

1. At the end of the last row, knot the beading thread to the warp. Weave back three rows and knot again on the middle warp. Trim.

2. At each end of the necklace there are at least 2-in. free warp threads. Cut them near the end of the loom. Thread each warp thread in the needle and weave back into the finished rows. Knot and trim.

D. Make a bead-and-loop fastener

1. Plan your colors for the fastener. Thread the needle with 6 in. of beading thread. Tie to the middle warp of the second row of beads from one end. Weave to the outside of the second row, back through the bottom bead of the first row. String three #3 beads, the 1/2-in. bead, three more #3 beads, go back through 1/2-in. bead and the first three #3 beads. Weave the thread back into the necklace, knot, and trim.

Knot + Trim

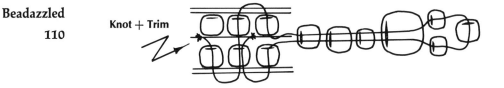

2. Thread the needle again with 6 in. of thread. Tie to the middle warp of the second row of the other end. Weave to the outside of the second row, back through the bottom bead of the first row. String one #3 bead, 22 seed beads, and go back through the #3 bead. Weave the thread back into the necklace, knot, and trim.

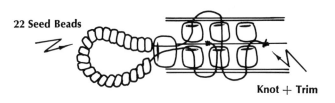

22 Seed Beads

Knot + Trim

E. Weaving the pendant

1. Look at chapter on bead messages. On graph paper, plan your design. The pendant could be about 16 beads long and 9 wide, but you can make your own dimensions.

2. Set up the loom. The number of warp threads should be one more than the number of beads in a row.

3. Weave in the same way you did the necklace. The first row is the hardest. Be careful to keep the needle under the warp when moving back to front and over the warp when moving front to back.

4. End old threads, start new ones, and finish the beading thread in the same way you did the necklace.

5. Cut the warp threads and knot them close to the beads. When you trim, leave a 1/2-in. thread.

F. Backing the pendant

1. Measure and cut out a piece of cotton backing 3/8 in. longer on each dimension than the pendant.

2. Tuck and hem to the same size as the pendant.

3. Iron the backing.

4. Sew the backing to the back side of pendant. Start with an edge without the warp threads to tuck in. Sew the very edge of the backing to the outer warp or weaving thread of the pendant. Make a stitch between every bead so that loose warp threads won't pull out later.

Outer Warp Thread

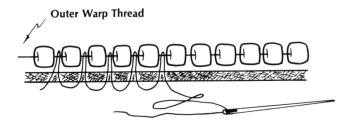

G. Weaving the necklace and pendant together

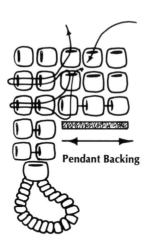

Pendant Backing

1. Place the pendant so that the left edge lines up with the third row of beads in from the loop end of the necklace.

2. Thread the needle with 12 in. of nylon thread.

3. Knot the end to the warp thread at the top of the second row of the pendant.

4. Weave to the outside. Weave up the third row of the necklace, over the end warp thread, back down through the third row of beads, through the second bead of the pendant, back up through the fourth row of the necklace, over the end warp thread, back down through the fourth row of the necklace, through the third bead of the pendant, and so forth. Finish by weaving the thread into the pendant, knotting, and trimming.

SOROBAN
ANALOG
COMPUTER

EQUIPMENT YOU WILL NEED:

Tape measure
Wood vise
Wood saw
Electric or hand drill
Drill bits; 1/16 and 9/32 (or 1/4)
Center punch
Hammer
60 wt. sandpaper

MATERIALS YOU WILL NEED:

7/8-in. broomstick or dowel at least 15 in. long
1/4-in. dowel 36 in. long
Two pieces 1/4-in. plywood 10 3/4 in. long and 1 1/2 in. wide (A and B)
One piece 1/4-in. plywood 9 1/8 in. long and 1 1/2 in. wide (E)
Two pieces 1-in. pine (actually 13/16 in. thick) 3 in. long and
  1 1/2 in. wide (C and D)
Eight nails 1 in. long
Glue

● This is a difficult project best done as a group.

DIRECTIONS:

A. Making the frame

1. In end pieces C and D, cut a 1/4-in. notch parallel to the 1 1/2-in. side and 3/4 of an inch from one end. The notch should be at least 1/4-in. deep (a little deeper does not matter).

2. On one side of A mark with a pencil where the seven holes for the dowel rods should be drilled. Follow the diagram below. The centers should be in a perfectly straight line 5/16 in. from the top. The first and last center marks are 1 3/8 in. from the ends of A. Otherwise, centers are 1 in. from each other. With a center punch mark the exact point where you will drill each

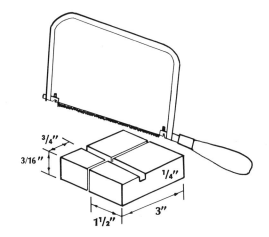

hole. Place B under A exactly flush. Drill each hole with a 1/8-in. bit. Keep the drill perpendicular to the board.

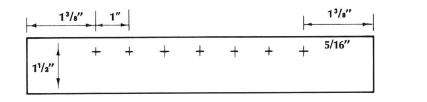

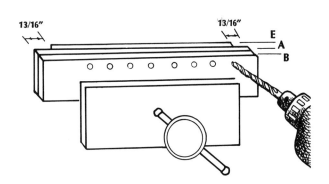

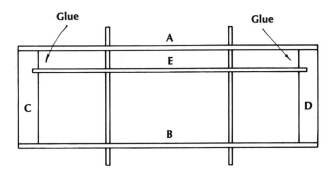

3. Center E behind A and B. The ends of E will be 13/16 in. from the ends of A and B. When the three pieces are aligned and flush at the top, put them in a vise tightly. Re-drill each hole in A and B with a 1/4-in. bit. Take off burrs with sandpaper.

4. Cut 1/4-in. dowel into two 18-in. lengths.

5. Glue A and B to C and D. Do this on a flat surface so that the corners are square. While the glue is wet, slip the two 1/4-in. dowels into the first and seventh holes to make sure the frame is aligned. Do *not* glue the dowels, only the sides. When the glue is dry, drill two 1/16-in. holes in the ends of A and B where they join C and D. Use these holes to nail the sides together.

6. Put glue in the notches of C and D. Insert E. Use dowels to align E with A and B. Wipe off excess glue. Allow to dry and remove dowels.

B. Making the bead counters

1. From a 7/8-in. broomstick or dowel, cut thirty-five wafers each 1/4 in. thick. (First put the dowel in the vise and cut a few 1/4-in. pieces. Since the saw wastes wood, you will have to judge how far apart to make the pencil marks in order to end up with 1/4-in. sections. A wood saw wastes about 1/16 in., so the pencil marks should be 3/16 in. apart. A jigsaw or hacksaw will waste less. Once you are confident you know the additional

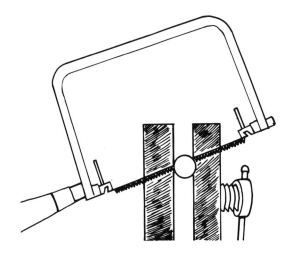

length needed for each 1/4-in. section, use a pencil and tape measure to make cut marks along the dowel for all thirty-five wafers.) Put the dowel in the vise and saw one wafer at a time, advancing the dowel after each cut.

2. Mark the center of each wafer with the center punch. Holding the wafer with pliers, drill a 1/8-in. hole. Then enlarge it with a 9/32-in. bit, or use a 1/4-in. bit and rotate the drill to enlarge the hole.

3. Bevel each bead counter by rubbing the edges on 60-weight sandpaper fixed to a flat surface. The sharper the bevel, the better. Irregularities are unimportant.

C. Finishing the Soroban

1. Cut nine lengths 3 1/2 in. each from the 1/4-in. dowel. These are the rods of the abacus.

2. Put a rod through the first hole of B. Slip on four counters. Put the rod through the first hole of the partition E. Add the fifth counter. Insert the rod in the first hole in A. Repeat for the other eight rods.

3. Glue the ends of the rods in A and B. Be careful to keep the glue off the bead counters.

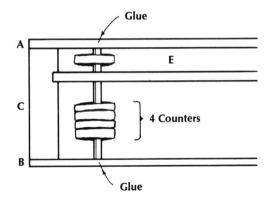

BEAD-EMBROIDERED NOTEBOOK COVER

EQUIPMENT YOU WILL NEED:

Scissors

Embroidery needle

Ruler

**Embroidery hoop or a small picture frame or a cardboard
carton with the bottom cut out**

MATERIALS YOU WILL NEED:

Indian Head cotton, drill cloth, or basketweave linen

Small notebook with stiff cover

**Two index cards (3 in. x 5 in. for notebooks under 6 in. high,
4 in. x 6 in. for larger sizes)**

Masking tape

White glue

Two colors embroidery floss (one same color as major color of beads)

Two packets seed beads, one mixed colors, one a single color

DIRECTIONS:

1. Cut a piece of cotton or linen fabric the size of the notebook's covers and glue to back and front of notebook. (This is your backing.)

2. Cut another piece the length and width of the open notebook, adding three inches to each measurement.

3. Place this piece of fabric in the hoop or thumbtack it on the frame or carton.

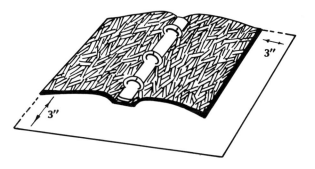

4. If this is a first try, create a design as you go along. Mark off the size of the front cover with chalk or light pencil dots. If you are an experienced embroiderer, draw your design directly on the fabric. Or transfer a more complicated design by copying the design onto tissue paper, which you sew with big basting stitches to the right side of the fabric. (The beads can then be sewn on through the tissue paper. The tissue paper is torn away and the basting stitches pulled out.)

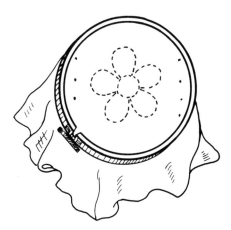

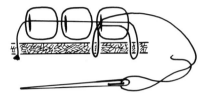

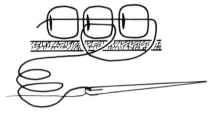

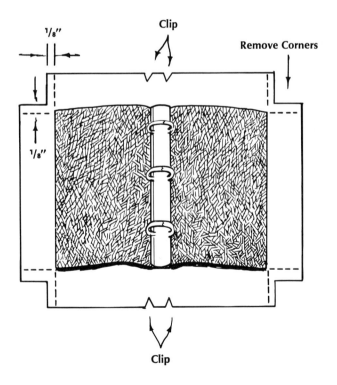

1/8"

1/8"

Clip

Remove Corners

Clip

5. Thread the needle with two strands of floss, knot the ends, and pass the needle up from the bottom of the fabric.

6. Slip three of the beads down to the end of the thread, settle them in place, and bring the needle back down through the fabric. (The stitch should be close enough so the thread does not extend beyond the end of the bead, yet loose enough so the beads lie evenly and do not pucker the fabric.)

7. Bring the needle back up close to where you passed it down and make a backstitch through the last bead. String another group of beads on the needle and repeat step 6.

8. To finish off, sew down through the fabric, up through the next-to-the-last bead, and double stitch through a few more beads. Then knot the thread on the underside and clip.

9. Place open notebook, rings up, on center of fabric.

10. Make two clips in the fabric on the top and bottom edges where the notebook's sides hinge; fold them under the notebook.

11. At each of the outside corners clip out a rectangle of the fabric that extends past the book corners, leaving 1/8 inch beyond the notebook's vertical edge.

12. To the inside of the front and back covers fold top and bottom margins; secure in place with masking tape.

13. Turn in the corner of each end margin diagonally, tucking in the extra 1/8 in. fabric to make a smooth corner. Then fold end margin to inside of notebook cover. Stitch down. Remove pieces of tape.

14. Lay corner of index card (plain side showing) 1/2–1 in. from the corner of the inside of front cover; trim even with inner border of fabric. Glue down. Repeat on back cover.

15. Make a beaded edging. (This can be done with one or several colors of beads. If you are edging all in one color, use the major color so you have plenty of beads.) Start at any hinge. Sewing with double strands of embroidery floss, draw thread out through crease of fabric (as in diagram), then through two beads, back through crease of fabric the width of bead away, and out again. Repeat procedure along entire border. End by knotting thread just inside the cover.

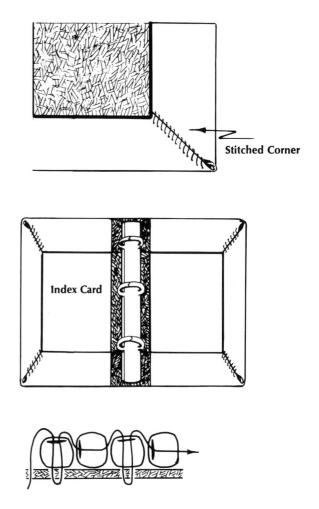

Stitched Corner

Index Card

● Try combining the bead embroidery with standard embroidery stitches like the satin or stem stitch. The beads also combine well with sequins and small felt decorations.

BEAD ROSE

EQUIPMENT YOU WILL NEED:

A measuring tape or yardstick
Small wire cutters or old kitchen scissors
Pair of long-nose pliers
Two small bowls
A few thumbtacks

MATERIALS YOU WILL NEED:

One bunch small seed beads, in yellow, pink, red, lavender, or
  white, size 11/0, already strung
One pack small transparent seed beads, green, size 11/0,
  already strung
One spool #28 galvanized stringing wire, green or silver, for flowers
One spool #26 wire for leaves
White enamelled wire if you are making a white rose
One length #16 stem wire, 9 in.
Roll of dark-green floral tape
Block of florist's clay

● Beading flowers is for patient, careful fingers. Your first rose *petal* may take up to an hour session. Later petals go faster. Work in a well-lighted area at least 3 ft. x 2 ft. If you do your beading over a large piece of felt you can easily retrieve dropped beads, which are easiest to pick up with a spoon. Keep your equipment on a tray for moving easily out of the way.

DIRECTIONS:

A. Separating the bunch

1. Hold the bunch of beads by the knotted tuft.

2. Select a strand that has some string showing at the top and gently pull one end loose.

3. Push all but the end bead up the thread. Tie the end bead with a single overhand knot. Find the other end and pull it out of the bunch. Knot the last bead on the end in the same way you knotted the first. Lay the strand in front of you.

4. Repeat until you have four of the colored strands of beads separated and closed with knotted beads. This is to ensure that no beads will be lost as you work.

5. Put the rest of the bunch in a saucer.

B. Stringing

1. Open a spool (which one depends on whether you are making petals or leaves) and unwind 3 ft. of wire. Push a thumb tack into the tip of the spool and wind the wire once or twice around the tack. Cut off the bead knotted at one end of one strand.

2. To thread the beads on the wire, place the strand along the top of your index finger, the open end toward your fingernail. Hold the string taut in-between crotch of thumb and fingers.

3. Using the wire as a needle, slide the end of the wire through as many beads on index finger as possible. Pull out the string as you transfer the beads from string to wire. Skip beads whose holes are too small.

4. When you have transferred the several strands onto the wire, you will have enough beads to complete several petals or leaves.

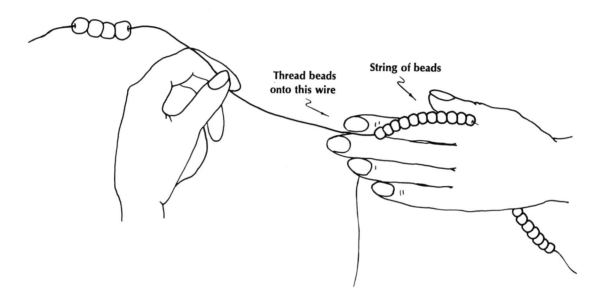

Thread beads onto this wire

String of beads

C. Beading

1. Push the beads down and unwind enough wire so there is 15 in. of bare wire showing at top of the beaded section of wire.

2. Make a tight double loop at the end of the wire so the beads don't fall off.

3. Beading is done from the spool. You don't cut the wire until you have finished the petal or leaf.

4. Place the spool at your left before beginning to bead. You will work with the piece of wire that is showing above strung beads.

5. Beads already strung on wire will be called Beaded Wire in these instructions. Before beginning, read section D to find out exactly how many beads to use for each petal and leaf. Then return to number 6 and start beading.

6. Slide the beginning group of beads (you will find out how many in section D) up to 2 in. below the wire knot. Holding these beads in place, double 8 in. of the wire into a loop 4 in. long. The loop is now between the beginning group of beads and the

spool. This beginning group of beads is the center row of the leaf or petal. Make a triple wind under the beads, tight enough to make a firm anchor.

7. Add rows of beads in the following way: holding the stem down, take enough beads from Beaded Wire to make the next row (each row has a few more beads than the previous one). Bring beads up the left side of the center row of beads. Stretch the spool wire over the front of the center row. Twist across the front and around the back of the center wire. There should be no beads on the part of the wire that is twisted around the center row. Then add beads down the right side of the center row. Fit beads closely alongside the first center row. (One bead too few will leave a gap with bare wire showing. One too many will make the petal loose.) Work should feel close and tight. Complete the first row by twisting the spool wire across the front of the center wire, around the back of the petal, and returning the wire across the front of the petal. Note that the spool wire goes straight across the Beaded Wire. This makes the petal round. Use pliers to straighten out any kinks as you work. Each time you add a row of beads, bring the beads of the spool wire up and fit closely, wrapping over, around the back of the stem, and down again so the wire from the spool encircles the stem wire.

8. Continue working around the petal until the required number of

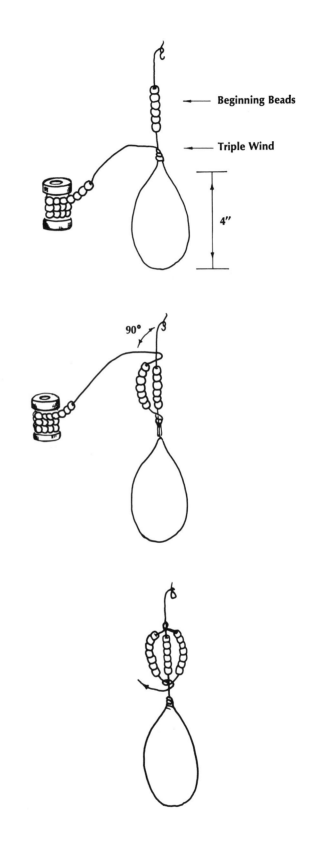

Beginning Beads

Triple Wind

4"

90°

rows have been completed. Always twist in the same direction. Let remaining beads slide back toward the spool each time you add a row. It is not necessary to count how many beads are on a row after the center row is completed. Rotate your petal with the same side facing you at all times. In this way more wire will show on the reverse side than on the front. (To repeat: the twist of wire goes over the front of the wire stem, around the back, and in a full circle again to position the next row.) The pattern always requires an uneven number of rows—the stem counts as one row. Each additional circle of beads adds two rows.

9. When the last row of a petal is complete, wind wire around the base of the stem, directly under the beads, three times. Cut the wire off close and with pliers press the tail end flush with loop stem. Cut the center wire 1/4 in. above the top of the finished leaf or petal. With your fingers, bend this 1/4 in. down the back of the petal.

10. Straighten the 4-in. loop, which you will use later to assemble the flower. You will have some beads left over on the Beaded Wire. You use these for the next petal. If you do not have enough beads for the next petal, string them on now. Before beginning the next petal give yourself 15 in. of bare wire at the top as you did for the first petal. Don't forget to knot the wire at the open end right away, so the beads on the Beaded Wire will not slide off. Repeat directions six through ten.

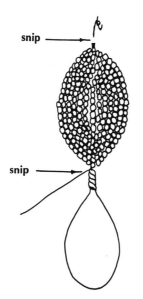

snip

snip

D. Pattern

1. Petals: make two with center row of six beads, five rows across; make two with center row of six beads, seven rows across; make three with center row of six beads, nine rows across; make three with center row of six beads, eleven rows across; make five with center row of six beads, fifteen rows across. You will have a fifteen petal rose. (Make the biggest petals as tight as you can. They are the hardest.)

2. Leaves: make one with center row of six beads, nine rows across;

make two with center row of six beads, eleven rows across; make two with center row of six beads, thirteen rows across. For the leaves, twist the wire the same as you did for the petals at the *base* of the leaf. But at the top of the leaf make a different kind of twist to make the leaf pointed. When the second row is alongside the center row of beads, add two extra beads before crossing the Beaded Wire over the center row of beads. Cross the top of the wire at an upward angle. This brings the Beaded Wire to a higher point than the previous row. Complete the row of beads down the right side. At the bottom make a horizontal twist. Trim each leaf by cutting the left side of the loop at the base of the beads. This makes a long stem.

3. Calyx: make six with center row of six beads, five rows across. Point the tops of the calyx leaves as you did for the other leaves. Trim so one long wire extends, as you did for the leaves.

E. Assembly

1. Place the two smallest petals (five rows) in an interlocking position and twist their stems together. Add the next size (seven rows) around this center, one at a time, opposite each other. The front of each petal will face inward. With pliers, twist the stems as petals are added. As you add petals, trim loop stems so that some are longer than others. This tapers the final stem. For each petal, leave at least two inches of stem wire below the beads. Cut off the unneeded stem wire. Add the larger petals (nine, eleven, and fifteen rows) one size at a time, working around the flower and overlapping slightly.

2. The parts of the calyx are added one at a time with faces up against the backs of the petals. Now twist all the stems together. Wrap all the stem wires in one direction.

3. Wrap the flower stems with florist's tape. Stretch the tape slightly. Wrap the stem diagonally, smoothly.

4. Wrap the leaves in the same way.

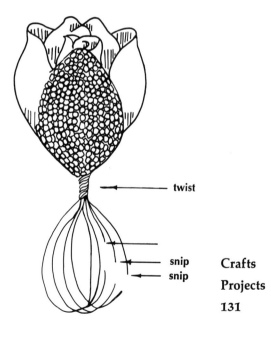

twist

snip
snip

5. Take 9 in. of #16 stem wire. With pliers bend 1 in. at the end at a right angle. Stick the bent wire through the flower stems, front to back. Fold it down into a hook.

6. Tape the flower stems to the #16 wire stem diagonally, tightly, smoothly. At the end leave 1/2 in. extra tape. Mold this to cover the end of the wire.

7. Place the leaf stems behind the stem wire. Tape these on in the same way.

8. After the flower is assembled, bend the petals and leaves with your fingers to give them a natural look.

9. Stick the stem of the flower in a block of florist's clay that has been fitted into the bottom of a vase.

10. Display in a vase. Under a lamp or in sunlight, the leaves will glow.

APPENDIX
INDEX
PHOTO
CREDITS

APPENDIX

MAIL-ORDER BEADS

The following is a list of businesses that sell beads by mail order. Each establishment carries a wide variety of beads, from inexpensive to expensive, and most will supply a catalogue upon request:

Beads and More   (No gold or silver beads)
7117 Third Avenue
Scottsdale, Arizona 85251

Freed Company
415 Central Avenue, NW
Albuquerque, New Mexico 87103

Glori Bead   (No catalogue available)
172 West 4th Street
New York, New York 10011

Sheru
49 West 38th Street
New York, New York 10018

Walbead   (Catalogue price $2.00)
38 West 37th Street
New York, New York 10018

INDEX

Index
142

PHOTO CREDITS

Courtesy of The American Museum of Natural History, pp. 15, 18, 19, 59.

Courtesy of Wendy Chesebrough, p. 26.

Courtesy of The Corning Museum of Glass, Corning, New York, p. 10.

Courtesy of *Essence* Communications Inc., Copyright 1980, p. 82.

Courtesy of Joshua Green and the Metropolitan Museum of Art Costume Institute, p. 78.

Courtesy of the Horniman Museum and Library, Forest Hill, England, pp. 40, 75.

Courtesy of Jonathan J. Lanman, p. 38.

Courtesy of the Metropolitan Museum of Art. All rights reserved, p. 53.

Collection of the Newark Museum, p. 56.

Courtesy of The Royal Museum of Fine Arts, Copenhagen, Denmark, p. 7.

Courtesy of The Netherlands Open Air Museum, pp. 46, 47, 49.

Courtesy of Dr. H. S. Schoeman, p. 31.

Courtesy of the Schomburg Center for Research in Black Culture, New York Public Library Astor, Lenox and Tilden Foundations, p. 43.

Courtesy of Mr. Tokuzumi, Nippon Steel Corporation, Tokyo, Japan, p. 64.

Courtesy of the Tomoe Soroban Company, Tokyo, Japan, p. 69.

Line drawings by Loren Bloom appear on pages 3, 23, 87, 91, 95, 101, 103, 104, 105, 107, 109, 110, 111, 112, 113, 115, 116, 117, 119, 121, 122, 123, 125, 128, 129.